Into Their Skin (both now and then)
writing biblical and historical skits, scripts, and monologues

Into Their Skin (both now and then)

writing biblical and historical
skits, scripts, and monologues

for homeschool, Christian schools,
youth groups and churches

Copyright June 2020 Carolyn Wing Greenlee

Layout: Dan Worley

ISBN 978-1-887400-60-2

Earthen Vessel Productions
www.earthen.com

Dedication
To my dear sons, John and Thomas,
who started it all

Introduction

Real people in real encounters with the Living God—the Bible abounds with them. But how do they relate to us? What can we learn from them? They seem so remote—ancient tales from a far away land. In some ways, they can seem as unreal as King Arthur and the knights of the Round Table.

Skits, scripts, and monologues based on biblical accounts can help your students get into the skins of the individuals who walked the Earth and made history thousands of years ago, and find, perhaps, unexpected life and truth, and deal with issues they hadn't considered.

This book began as a combination of two courses on biblical and historical script writing that I wrote for my classes at a Christian school in the 1980s.

The first section focuses on what I call "reversal scripts," where the people involved make different choices from what we know they did in reality. Your students get to contemplate and then explore the answer to this question, "But what if?" But what if Saul chose to go fight Goliath instead of sending David, a teenager, to do what he had no courage to do himself? How would their lives have been different?

I also included a script of an historical account because sometimes it's easier for students to see alternatives to the outcomes by giving them a chance to identify the moral and ethical issues from a fresh point of view.

The second part of this book is on writing biblical monologues, which offers opportunities to investigate the internal workings of the beliefs and reasonings that led to the character's actions. Lot's wife is an example. Why did she look back?

I want to equip you to guide your students in ways that help them gain insight, not only into the lives of the people whose actions were reported in biblical and historical accounts, but also into their own in the twenty-first century.

In the following pages, you will find skits, scripts, monologues, examples from my students, and many suggestions of subject matter available in the Bible.

Your students might not be old enough to write scripts, but they can make them up and talk about them. Or you could write some, collaborate with your students, or read them the ones in this book. A little music (taped or live) at an appropriate moment can add drama and impact.

Whether you are using these exercises as a course for writing or using the ideas for discussions, devotions, or impromptu skits, I hope you find excitement as you delight in teaching the children these things, for there is no greater privilege than to reveal the Truth of God to them in ways which He, Himself, will open to you as you seek to make Him better known.

Enjoy your journey!

Carolyn Wing Greenlee
Kelseyville, CA

but what if?
Writing Reversal Scripts

What if Saul had gone to fight Goliath?
What if Achan hadn't taken the spoils from Jericho?
What if Ananias and Sapphira had repented before the Lord?

The truth of God is fathomless, yet we can become superficial in our reading of His Word; we can be bereft of greater, richer depths of understanding simply because of the familiarity of the stories we think we know so well. Reversal Scripts help us see these familiar accounts in a new light. It's helpful to review the scriptural account for content and detail before reading the reversal script.

Here is an example of a reversal script written by one of my students, my son Thomas.

Saul and David
by Thomas Ramirez
Age: 16 years
(1 Samuel 17)

SCENE: Saul is sitting on a small throne inside his royal tent. He is tapping impatiently on one of the arms of the throne. A messenger enters.

Messenger: Your Majesty, David, son of Jesse, whom you sent for is here.
Saul: (sits up and tries to look royal) Very good. Send him in.(Messenger leaves, then comes back with David, who bows before the throne, head down. Saul motions messenger to leave.) I hear you want to battle Goliath. (David looks up.)
David: Let no man's heart fail because of him. Your servant will go and fight with this Philistine.
Saul: You are able to go and fight with him? After all, you are just a youth. He has been a man of war since he was a youth.

3

David: Your servant used to keep his father's sheep, and when a lion came and took a lamb out of the flock, I went after it, and struck it, and delivered the lamb from its mouth. And when it arose against me, I caught it by its beard and struck and killed it. Your servant has killed both lion and bear, and this uncircumcised Philistine will be like one of them, seeing he has defied the armies of the living God! The Lord, who delivered me from the paw of the lion and from the paw of the bear, will deliver me from the hand of the Philistine.

Saul: (sits forward on his throne, looks intently at David) Are you saying that you have enough faith to go fight this giant—that you trust God so much that you will risk your life on that trust?

David: Yes, my lord, it is as you say.

Saul: The Lord has sent you to rebuke my unbelief. Am I not king over the Lord's people? Do I not stand head and shoulders over all grown men in Israel? Was I not anointed by God through the prophet Samuel?

David: It would be right for my lord to have the honor of defeating this idolatrous enemy, to prove there is still the living God in Israel.

Saul: (standing up) Yes, David, I will go and fight this Philistine. What is a giant in comparison with the living God? (strides over to tent flap) Guard! Call my armor bearer. Have him ready my armor! (strides back to David) Arise, David! For the service done by you to me in obeying God's orders, I will call you my son, my crown prince. Samuel was right in anointing you as the next king.

Narrator: God could have used Goliath as a source of victory to Saul. He could have blessed Saul by defeating the Philistine army, but because of Saul's unbelief, God was not able to show His power through the king. Saul's lack of trust in God held back His power. Because of his faith in God, David defeated Goliath, an act that set up a jealousy in Saul that haunted him for the rest of his life.

- The End -

Reversal

You notice that the action begins in the familiar way. David offers to go out against Goliath. The reversal comes when Saul recognizes his own attitude of faithlessness. He decides to trust God. The story has a happy and satisfying ending...until the narrator steps in and reminds the audience of the consequences of Saul's actual choice.

Many times we read these accounts without ever considering that the people involved in them could have acted differently.

—Sarai could have told her husband, "I love you, Honey, but I won't lie for you," and Abram could have decided to trust God to deliver them in a foreign land. Instead, he put his wife, and the promise of a people chosen by God to bring forth Messiah, the Savior of the world, in jeopardy. (Genesis 12:10-20)

—Lying in the dust on the Damascus road, Saul could have rebelled rather than receive the calling of God. (Acts 9:1-22)

—When others told him to hush, Blind Bartimeus could have sat back down in discouragement rather than lift his voice to cry out to Jesus for his healing. (Mark 10:46-52)

—Herod could have told Salome that the head of John the Baptist was in the half of the kingdom he didn't promise her. (Luke 9:9)

—Lot's wife could have kept her eyes straight ahead. (Genesis 13:5-13)

Choices, Choices

Because we know the course of events in these stories, reversal scripts offer an opportunity to consider, by logical extension, how a single choice can change the course of a life and even alter the course of history. You can use the reversal format for impromptu skits or dialogues or discussions.

In the case of David and Goliath, what other possibilities are there? David could "chicken out." Or he could let Saul talk him into using his armor. Or he could go out against Goliath with a tank and a machine gun.

Students who worked with reversal scripts found that they began to regard Biblical characters as real human beings—people like themselves who had to make choices under pressure—people who did not always make the best choices. By changing the choices of biblical characters, students had the opportunity to project what the results would have been, good or bad.

Here is another example, this one written by my son John.

Ananias and Sapphira
by John Ramirez
Age: 17
(Acts 5)

Ananias: (He enters carrying a bag of money.) Well, Peter, we sold our property as we said we would. Here's all the money for the work of the ministry—eight thousand dollars!

Peter: Ananias, are you sure that's how much you sold it for?

Ananias: Yes. I mean, uh, well (Peter assumes a stern expression.) I mean, uh, well...

Peter: (quietly, but sternly) Ananias...

Ananias: (breaking down, speaking in a whisper) No. We sold it for twelve thousand. I just thought...well, it sold better than we thought it would and we thought that...well...

Peter: You thought that you'd lie to the Holy Spirit?!

Ananias: No!

Peter: Didn't you? While the property was yours, you could do with it what you wanted. When you say you're giving it all to God, you'd better do just that!

Ananias: But we needed the money. We were buying a new house and...and...

Peter: Didn't you think of the consequences? Is the new life you have received in Christ that cheap to you that you would cast it away for mere money? Would you sell an eternity with God for four thousand dollars?

Ananias: How could I have been so foolish, so greedy? I have sinned against God and against you. I have dishonored myself, my wife, and, most of all, my God!

Peter: Would you like to spend some time in prayer? (gesturing off stage. Ananias leaves. Sapphira rushes in with a bag of money.)

Sapphira: Peter! Peter! Where is he? Is he...dead?

Ananias: (entering) Here I am, Sapphira!

Sapphira: Oh, Ananias! I thought you were...I thought you had...

Ananias: No, Sapphira. I told him the truth.

Sapphira: Oh! I'm so glad! I was afraid for you—for us—just thinking about what we almost did. All I could think of was how much money it was. A new house, a better vineyard, maybe an Egyptian servant girl. Then I realized Who we were stealing it from. I couldn't bear to think what would happen if we actually went through with it! (shudders) I brought the rest of the money.

Ananias: Thank you, Sapphira. Peter, I now give the full amount of twelve thousand dollars to the work of the ministry with a clean conscience. (starts to leave)

Peter: Ananias, our God is an all-consuming fire. But if we ask God's forgiveness and repent, He will cleanse us. Go in peace.

Narrator: How many lives would have gone differently if this were the outcome, we shall never know. They would have enjoyed healthy, productive lives, enriched with the blessings of God. They would have been filled with peace and love and joy. But we shall never know. Ananias and Sapphira openly lied to the Holy Spirit and were immediately struck dead for their iniquity. Our holy Lord keeps His Word with His people, and demands that we do the same.

- The End -

Evaluation

The "moral of the story" narration at the end of the script will carry the perspective of the writer. In this play, notice that the emphasis is on the requirement of holiness.

Holiness is certainly an important part of our relationship with God, but "Ye shall be holy because I am holy" can be read different ways, and the inflection totally changes the meaning. Try speaking it as an imperious decree. Now try it as a gentle word, reassuring the listener that God's holiness results in our own—as children become like the parents they respect and love.

At the time John wrote this script, we were attending a very legalistic church whose god was demanding, exacting, and almost impossible to please. One misstep and you were gone. There was no grace and no forgiveness unless you came crawling back on broken glass.

In that kind of doctrine, you could lose your salvation for lying to the Holy Spirit, and immediate death and Hell were the consequences. There was no room for failure, or the mistakes that happen as you're learning to walk in the Spirit and not after the flesh . Salvation had to be earned and maintained—a kind of Eternal Probation—until you made it, by death, into Heaven. And there was never a guarantee that you would make it because, at any moment, you could blow it and be lost forever.

There are still churches that teach these doctrines. The word for this apostasy is Legalism. It was characteristic of the Pharisees in Jesus' day. It says I can be righteous by doing these things. I can establish my own righteousness before God instead of God's establishing His own righteousness in me through Christ.

Since the emphasis is on external performance, people under this system either lie (because no one can be holy through personal exertion) which leads to hypocrisy, or blindness to what God's true holiness entails.

Of course, this fits with Confucianism, which is all about keeping the rules, so I truly believed I had, at long last, become the good girl my father kept telling me he wanted me to be. I was self-righteous, not righteous or grateful because of what Jesus did for me. Legalism makes you proud and causes you to look down on other people. And it really satisfies the flesh!

If, on the other hand, you lacked the discipline to keep all the rules, or if you were, like my son John, too honest to pretend he didn't like girls, you were labeled rebellious, carnal, worldly, willfully wicked and sinful. The Word of God was used as a weapon of condemnation, and you can see the effect it had on my son.

Reading this script more than thirty years after leaving that church, I shudder to see the kind of harsh, demanding doctrine that overshadowed the life of my son: you are acceptable only as long as you do everything right. Toe The Line or Drop Dead.

I decided to leave this script the way it was originally written because it is a good example of the way our attitudes and beliefs are evidenced in our expressions. Your students' writing will reveal much of how they feel about God. If you see something amiss, you will have opportunity to bring them more perfect understanding of the God who loves them, and will not forsake them through all their flailings and failings.

The Bible doesn't say Ananias and Sapphira lost their salvation by this deceit, because they had already chosen to believe Jesus had paid for all of their sins,. Salvation was theirs by the grace of God, not by performance. However, they lost a lifetime of growing in increasingly deep and beautiful fellowship with the Creator of the universe, and the fulfillment that is possible in a human life no other way.

Contemporary Form

In the contemporary form, reversal scripts make use of the fast-paced talk of Twenty-first Century media. It is important to choose a well-known biblical account because the main element in this format is irony. Notice that, at the end, no narrator appears to relate facts of the actual event.

News Flash!
by Thomas Ramirez
Age: 16

News Flash #1 (Genesis 6)
Newsman: Earlier today, you might have noticed large drops of water falling out of the sky. Our meteorologist, Noah, told us not to worry, and that it would "rain," as he put it, for forty days and forty nights. Also, it might be noted that the "Tomorrow Show" has been canceled.

News Flash #2 (Judges 6)
Newsman: Earlier today, three hundred bagpipe carrying men were arrested for noise pollution after they reportedly smashed Ming vases and flashlights over the heads of their Midianite oppressors.

Announcer: And now, back to our commercials, which are already in progress.

- The End -

Contemporary Issues

Reversal scripts also afford a vehicle for presenting contemporary situations— tribulations and afflictions common to the Christian life. Pressure to deviate from the Plan of God (especially from family members,) can be effectively presented in biblical situations in which there is one against many—for example, Rahab's family as they assemble in her house, awaiting the army of the Lord God of Israel. (Joshua 2) Human logic, sweetly reasonable, can cause Rahab to doubt, waver, and ultimately make the choice which leads to the destruction of them all.

"Why a scarlet cord? Honestly, Rahab! You have no imagination! Purple is the 'in' color this year. Don't be such a stick-in-the-mud. Get with it, girl!"

"Are you sure they asked for a scarlet cord? Where are we going to find such a thing? I saw a rope in the back closet. Won't that do just as well? I mean, what difference can it make? A rope, a cord, it's all the same."

"You really believe you can trust those guys? Why, they were spies! They probably planned to come back and torture us all. What makes you think you can trust them? Let's not hang anything in the window at all. We could go out the back. They'll never know."

I noticed the account reports that Rahab wasn't taking any chances. After the spies left her house, she bound the scarlet cord in her window (Joshua 2:21). My guess is that she did it immediately, just to make sure nothing went amiss. And because she did, her whole family was saved, and she, herself, became a special part of Messiah's genealogy, being one of the women mentioned by name, and also the grandmother of Boaz, the kinsman redeemer who married Ruth, another Gentile woman. Boaz and Ruth would have a very important great grandson, David, the one who would be called a man after God's own heart.

In Times of Distress, Duress, and Fear

We are called to be epistles read of all men—lighting and salting the world, following our Lord Jesus, believing His trustworthy faithfulness even in the most frightening of circumstances. The result? Joy. Peace. Security. Satisfaction.

At Antioch, believers were so obviously fulfilling that charge that the people called them "Christ-ins" and yet we are frequently robbed of the joy of moving in this world-changing, startling kind of Christian life. Why? Is it because it costs too much, hurts too much, it takes too much time and effort? Is it just because it's unfamiliar, inconvenient, uncomfortable, offensive, politically unpopular, exclusive, inflammatory, restrictive, or too old-fashioned? Are we nervous about surrendering all to Jesus because we're not sure what He'll do to us? Maybe send us to Africa? Does the word "surrender" represent defeat and resignation to the control of a powerful conquerer? Or are we simply stampeded into fear and doubt as an array of facts rises up—an army of overwhelming "realities" asserting themselves against what God tells us is true?

Choices Under Duress

There are many glorious victories reported in the book of Acts. We read them and accept them as courageous deeds of people who were far stronger and better than we. Reversal scripts remind us that they, too, had to make choices under duress—and that they could have just as easily made worse ones.

Paul and Silas
(Acts 16:16-40)

Paul: (shaking one manacled wrist ruefully) This isn't exactly what I expected.

Silas: Yeah.

Paul: We would probably do well to reevaluate where we're going.

Silas: Yeah.

Paul: Did you ever think it'd come to this? I wanted to serve the Lord, but…

Silas: Yeah.

Facts have a way of looking unalterable, but God's Truth supersedes circumstances just as the Law of Lift supersedes the Law of Gravity. If that is so, then faith can manifest as confidence in God's ability to do what He says He will, no matter how it looks to us at the time. Perspective from God's point of view is a powerful way of changing our view of reality.

Paul was in prison when he wrote that in his weakness, God's strength was made perfect. Do we believe that in our own lives? When I'm weakest, is that when His strength is most powerful on my behalf?

Thrown into jail, beaten and manacled in stocks, for Paul and Silas the facts were indisputable, the outlook grim. There wasn't much chance of being set free, yet they submitted the whole matter to God, recognizing that the God who created the universe could create a solution to their problem.

At midnight, "Paul and Silas were praying and singing hymns to God," singing their faith in His character and ability. And God shook them loose. The facts were no match for the truth that their God was a very present help in trouble.

Naming Fictitious Characters

There are cases when people are mentioned in the Bible but not named. What do you do if you want to write a skit involving any of those? In the script I wrote on Achan, I made up a name for his wife. However, since then I have learned that each Hebrew letter has a meaning, a picture, a number, and a musical note. If you know what the meaning of each letter is, you can read Hebrew. Consonants are not generally a part of Hebrew words; we add them so we can say them, which explains how you can get Jehovah or Yahweh out of YHWH, the I AM name of the God of the burning bush.

There is need for attention and intentionality in naming your characters. There's meaning in Hebrew beyond our understanding, so I don't recommend making up words. There are books of the names of everyone in the Bible and what they mean. It's better to find one that suits your storyline. It will also help the writing of the script because the meaning of the name will enrich the writing of the character.

Achan

I wrote *Achan* in 1986 while I was still attending the legalistic church. I rewrote it, and the comments which follow it, about a year after leaving the church. Having been brought up Taoist/Confucian, I didn't know what was wrong with my Christianity. All I knew was it was killing me. I started listening to other teachers, but it was hard to sort out ten years of intense study and indoctrination from what turned out to be apostasy.

When the Lord made it clear I was to leave that church, the leadership told me I was going to Hell because I was turning my back on the only church where I would hear the truth of God's requirements of holiness. I was suicidal for a year and a half.

But God sent me wonderful mentors to love me into the Land of the Living, showing me that the surprising consequence of a close, trusting, intimate relationship with Almighty God is obedience. I now choose to do God's will, not because I'm terrified of being rejected or discarded, but because I love Him so much. The more I value what He values, the more I align with His will, the closer I feel to Him and the happier I am, for in His presence is fullness of joy. There's nothing else even remotely like it.

Achan
by Carolyn Wing Greenlee
(Joshua 7)

CAST: Achan; his wife, Tirzah; four children

SCENE Achan walks in the door of his tent. He is laden with beautiful garments and jewels. His children crowd around excitedly. His wife, Tirzah, gives him a hug.

Achan: (handing items to each child) This is for you! And this is for you! And you too. And this (gives to the littlest one) is for you! Now go out and play. A man needs rest after a battle. (The children protest a little.) No, go on! I'll tell you all about it at supper. Yes, I promise! Go on! Go! Go! Let Papa catch his breath! (The children scamper off stage, admiring their gift.)

Tirzah: Achan! I'm so glad to see you! Here, sit down. Let me get you some cool water.

Achan: (dropping into a chair) Thank you, Tirzah. (slumps a moment while she is out, then remembers, jumps to his feet, ducks out of the tent, and reenters with something behind his back. Tirzah returns with a cup, looks for him in the chair, sees that he's not there, and turns to see him standing by the tent flap.)

Tirzah: (laughing lightly) Oh, you startled me!

Achan: (with a flourish presents her with a beautiful garment) And THIS is for you, my love!

Tirzah: (taking it carefully from his hand and holding it up to herself) It's, it's the most beautiful garment I've ever seen!

Achan: (proudly) I thought so, too.

Tirzah: (somewhat anxiously) Oh, Achan! Is it all right? I mean…

Achan (expansively) Yes! Of course it's all right! The LORD told us to take the livestock and spoils as booty for ourselves. Ai was loaded with them!

Tirzah: (quickly) Oh, I don't doubt your integrity, husband! That never crossed my mind! It was just that (hesitatingly) at Jericho…

Achan: At Jericho, He told us the spoil was His. At Ai, He told us it was ours. No problem, my love. Stop looking so anxious!

Tirzah: (relaxing, and admiring again the garment) All right. It is a beautiful gown. It's just that…well, our God is a consuming fire. I wouldn't want us…you…any of us, really, to dishonor Him.

Achan: Dishonor! No, My Dear! On the contrary! Jehovah must be quite pleased with us. We went to Ai with the good hand of the Lord upon us—in His full blessing. We routed the enemy in only a few hours' time—destroyed them easily and completely, and with not a single casualty on our side! Not one!

Tirzah: (eyes shining with joy) Oh, Achan! Not one casualty! Our Lord was truly with you! Forgive my fear!

Achan: (long pause, looking down, then speaking quietly) There is something I need to confess to you, though.

Tirzah: (listening, but still looking at the gown) Oh?

Achan: Yes. (long pause) I was tempted in Jericho,

Tirzah: (freezes without looking up) What do you mean?

Achan: I was looking through the rubble, you know, of the walls?

And I stepped over some loose rocks and saw a glint of gold. It was a wedge of gold, actually. And nearby were some shekels of silver. (musing almost to himself) Now, as I think back on it, it wasn't even a large wedge and there weren't many shekels, but it seemed like a vast amount at the time…

Tirzah: (scarcely breathing)) Go on…

Achan: That wasn't all. Some purple caught my eye and I looked to the left. There, partially buried in the rubble, was a silky Babylonian garment. I could just see it on you, Tirzah! I could imagine your expression when you saw it—the shine in your eyes.

Tirzah: (anxious, but controlling herself) Go on…

Achan: And so I reached for it (quickly) just to see it better, you understand!

Tirzah: (in horror) Oh, Achan! The Lord God said not even to touch the unclean thing! Oh, Achan!

Achan: Now, wait, Tirzah! Calm down!

Tirzah: (nearly in tears) Achan! Achan! Did you! Oh, PLEASE!

Achan: No.

Tirzah: (slumping) Oh, thank God!

Achan: (hanging his head) But I was sorely tempted, Tirzah. (She looks at him, tense again. He speaks earnestly.) At that moment, nothing seemed more important than bringing home that beautiful garment, that shiny silver and gold. At that moment, I forgot—no, I cast off—the commandment of my Lord God Jehovah. I willingly chose to covet what He had told us to abhor. (long pause) I kept thinking how beautiful you would look, how pleased you would be, how proud you would be…(hangs his head again and barely whispers) of…me.

Tirzah: Oh, my husband! How could you think I would be pleased by a transgression of the command of God? Didn't you realize that such a thing would destroy us—all of us? (Miserable, he shakes his head, "no.") Oh, Achan! The LORD whose eyes are in every place—would He not see the accursed thing? Did you think to deceive the Creator of the universe—the All-knowing, All-wise, All-POWERFUL HOLY God?

Achan: (looking up quickly, speaking entreatingly) At that moment, I thought only of you…(drops head) No. I thought only of myself. I sought to secure more of your love and favor by bringing you gifts.

Tirzah: (softer) I do not love you for the spoils of war you bring, my husband. I love you because you are a man of faith, a man of integrity—a man of God. Never never sacrifice your relationship with God for favor with me. Unless He is first in your life and mine, our love cannot last, for our life would be built on sand. (pause, then gently) But you didn't take it. You only thought to take it. It is no sin to be tempted—only to act upon the temptation. (Achan nods, head in hands)

Achan: Tirzah, I am most ashamed of this, that I would want to snatch for myself something outside of the will of God when He has always abundantly met our needs. What would cause me to doubt His wisdom? (looks down, long pause) The spoils in Ai were even richer than the ones in Jericho, and this garment even more beautiful than the one I saw before…but of course, in Jericho, I had no way of knowing…Just think. I could have been accursed!

Tirzah: (patting him reassuringly on the arm) I'm so thankful that you resisted—that you obeyed God! I don't know what I would have done if you hadn't….

Tirzah and Achan freeze. Narrator walks in front of them and addresses the audience.

Narrator: On the seventh day of the march around Jericho, Joshua commanded the people according to the instructions of the Lord, "And you, by all means keep yourselves from the accursed things, lest you become accursed when you take of the accursed things, and make the camp of Israel a curse, and trouble it."

What blessing could have been on the lives of Achan and his family had he chosen to obey! Instead, Achan "saw among the spoils a beautiful Babylonian garment, two hundred shekels of silver, and a wedge of gold," coveted them, and hid them in the earth under his tent. And it seemed that no one knew, and it seemed it could hurt no one. But, in Ai, thirty-six men were struck down in battle, grief ravaged the lives of their widows and children, and the hearts of the people melted and became like water.

If he had only waited, Achan could have had, by God's hand of blessing, what he snatched for himself in Jericho. Instead, "Joshua, and all Israel with him, took Achan the son of Zerah, the silver, the garment, the wedge of gold, his sons, his daughters, his oxen, his donkeys, his sheep, his tent, and all that he had, and they brought them to the Valley of Achor…So all Israel stoned him with stones; and they burned them with fire after they had stoned them with stones. They raised over him a great heap of stones, still there to this day."

- The End -

Evaluation

In a moment of temptation, Achan disregarded the explicit command of his God and took something outside of His will. Why? Why do we think God would withhold something good from us? These are questions you might ask your students. It's the fundamental issue old as the Garden of Eden: God is not good. He doesn't want you to have something that would be good for you, so you'd better take it for yourself. Don't worry. You shall not surely die.

I find it significant that, in the next battle, God intended to give all the booty to the Israelites. One of the enemy's strategies is to press us to take it now, thereby disrupting or destroying what God had planned to provide for us in His perfect timing, which always makes rich and adds no sorrow.

I love what these godly people taught me about the will of God.

Bryan Duncan says God has three answers to prayer: "Yes," "Not yet," and "I have something better."

Bob Cull told me, "No" is as good an answer as "Yes" if you know His heart.

And someone else (whose name I can't remember) said, "God's will is what we would always choose if we knew all the facts."

Why did God tell them to kill everyone, including women and children?

It's these types of Old Testament accounts that cause so many to turn away from the Bible with a shudder and either read only the

New Testament or think of God the Father and God the Son in terms of Bad Cop/Good Cop. But Jesus said they are exactly One. There is no difference in motivation or expression.

This issue is so important that I devoted an entire chapter to it in another book, What Can Wreck Your Child and What To Do About It. It's one of the major stumbling blocks Christians trip over in both Bible reading and relating to the Godhead. But for now, here are some factors that help explain the genocide that turns our stomachs and makes us wonder about the goodness of God.

The Canaanite religion involved the worship of Baal and a lot of other gods and goddesses. Sex with temple prostitutes was a big part of the worship as was child sacrifice, which is why the Lord ordered that every Canaanite be killed and burned. It reminds me of when there were smallpox epidemics. Things had to be burned in an attempt to protect the living from the devastating, contagious disease.

But why not let the children live?
There's a term in the medical field—miasm. It is a term for an inherited aberration that shows up in subsequent generations. An example is spina bifida, where the child is born with a hole in its spine. Somewhere up the family tree, an ancestor had syphilis, a sexually transmitted disease,.

The Bible says the sins of the fathers are visited upon the children to the third and fourth generation. This turns out to be more literal than we think. There are genetic aberrations that are passed down in badly transcribed DNA that show up in the offspring, and it's encoded into the very instructions of their genome.

There is a spiritual encoding that also gets passed down. The sins of the fathers are not necessarily diseases. Even traumas, such as famine, are transmitted. This was dramatically evidenced in the children of Holocaust survivors. Severe diseases and emotional and mental problems manifested in their children, even at a young age.

Spiritual wickedness is also passed down. Just as there are families of immense moral rectitude and strength (such as the Rechabite in Jeremiah 35), there are families notorious for their violence and cruelty. There are races of people too. The Waoranis of Eastern Ecuador were so vicious the other Ecuadorian tribes called them "Aucas," which means savages. So a child with a Canaanite bloodline would come loaded with inherited defilement and a culture where they, as adults, would worship by passing their own babies through the fire as living sacrifices burned alive to please a demon god.

But any child who dies before the age of accountability goes to Heaven. For the Canaanite children, that wouldn't be such a bad thing.

Talking with your students about these kinds of issues, helping them work through things that seem horrific to us, or that make no sense to our modern minds, can help them navigate a lifetime of confusing circumstances, building up their faith in God's goodness rather than letting it erode in the suspicion that He's not really good after all.

By the way, there is nothing in scripture that says Achan and his family all went to Hell because of his actions, though sin has a way of destroying more than the one who sinned. The Bible says every-thing in it is for our instruction, and certainly the picture of Achan and all he held dear buried under a heap of rocks is a striking illus-tration of a spiritual truth. Consequences are the result of choices and all of us have free will.

It also makes me so very, very grateful for Jesus, and the grace of God that offers forgiveness and redemption for all our transgres-sions. That amazing grace is what transforms us and restores us to fellowship with the living, holy God.

Historical Reversal Scripts

There is something about the printed page which carries a sense of the inexorable. History remains locked in black and white, forever whatever it was reported to be. It can also imply an element of inev-itability—that no matter who the players are, the outcome would be the same because human nature is the same.

Reversal scripts of non-biblical history help us view documented occurrences, not as inevitabilities set in stone, but as the result of choices made by regular human beings—choices which could have just as well been very different.

Achan sinned for luxury. What he took was not a necessity for life. But what if the need is more "legitimate"? What if the need is food?

The story of the Donner Party, a well-known historical horror, crowds us towards rationalizing ungodly choices. Shouldn't we do everything we can to preserve our lives?

To explore the results of this thinking further, I wrote a script on the Donner Party. I hope it will open good dialogue between you and your students, because the more we extricate ourselves from "the given" in society's norms and the more we evaluate life and death issues in the context of God's point of view, the better they will be able to live secure and strong no matter what comes their way.

In my script, I wanted to show different reactions of people in conditions of extreme suffering.

No names are given to these characters because the Donner Party had real people and these characters are fictitious. I didn't want any character to be associated with any of the actual members of the Donner group. Man 1 is a Christian whose faith increases through the trials. Man 2 is independent and self-reliant. He makes sure he gets what he needs, does not rely on God for anything, but also has the internal moral compass God put into each human being. Mother is a Bible-quoting Christian who has gone to church all her life, but has never addressed the real issues of living for Jesus or examining what those scriptures really mean.

Sadly, many Christians fold when God doesn't heal their loved one or protect them from hardship, or keep His promises according to their understanding of what His words mean. In my script, Mother's repetitions of, "my God shall supply," exhibit increasing deterioration of her faith in God's goodness. Convinced that God doesn't hear or care, she decides to take matters into her own hands.

The Donner Party
by Carolyn Wing Greenlee

CAST: Man 1, Man 2, Mother, Child

SCENE 1: Two men stand huddled against the wind. Nearby, a woman sits on a rock. A small child is lying on her lap. She bends over to shelter the child with her own body.

Man 1: I don't know how much more of this cold I can take. How many days has it been now?

Man 2: (listlessly) Who knows? Too many.

Child: (weakly) Mommy, I'm hungry.

Mother: (despairing, but soothing) I know, Honey. Mommy is, too.

Man 1: I wonder if they're looking for us? Think they might?

Man 2: Who knows? We weren't due for another couple weeks.

Mother: (alarmed) You mean they might not know we're stuck here in the snow?

Man 2: No, Ma'am. How would they know?

Mother: I just thought they could see by the sky…

Man 1: Ma'am, we're in a pass in the mountains far away from our destination. Sky's bound to look different from that far away. Chances are they don't even suspect anything's gone wrong.

Man 2: Yep. Think we're just moving along—horses and mules and…

Mother: (interrupting) Stop it!

Man 2: What's the matter, Ma'am? Mule meat stew not agree with you?

Mother: No. It was fine. I just didn't want to think about it.

Man 2: Well, it was better than starving at the time.

Mother: I just thought God would have provided another way.

Man 2: What way?

Mother: I don't know—maybe manna like He did in the wilderness. I mean, this is wilderness isn't it? He said He'd supply all our need. This is a need, isn't it? I mean, if we don't get something to eat, we'll all starve here. Wouldn't you say that was a legitimate need? He did manna for them. He could do it for us. Maybe even quail.

Man 2: (scoffing) Quail! Ma'am, God helps those who help themselves. So we ate the mules and we're still alive. That's all that matters to me.

Mother: (quiet for a moment, then looks up) Do you really think they think we're all right? Don't you think there's even a little chance they'll come looking for us?

Man 1: Not much. And, even if they did, the same snow that keeps us locked in can keep them locked out.

Mother: (looking back down) Oh. (long pause) So what do you think is going to happen to us?

Man 2: Most likely we'll starve.

Mother: Starve! But God said…

Man 2: (brutally) God's not here! Can't you see that? He's not going to bring manna or quail or even a jack rabbit. If He were going to, do you think He would have waited until now? Why didn't he do it before we had to kill our pack animals? How does He expect us to make it through the pass now?

Mother: But, "My God shall supply…"

Man 2: Has He? (Mother says nothing) Has He? (she drops her head)

Child: (weakly) Mommy…

Mother: Hush, child. I'm here.

Man 2: You're here, but where is God? If He cares so much, let's see Him fill the belly of that little one there. If He's such a loving God, how can He let her suffer? I've been a hard man all my life and I'll take what I deserve—I've never asked no man to pay my way. But that little one…

Mother: (dully) So we're just going to die. (pause) And nobody will ever know what happened to us. (pause) A slow painful death in the pass of a mountain range somewhere, who knows where, and nobody will ever know.

Man 2: Or care.

Mother: Or care…(dully) I never thought it would be like this… perishing in the wilderness with no one even aware to lift a prayer on my behalf to the Heavenly Father who…(somewhat bitterly) doesn't seem to care either.

Man 1: Now, Ma'am, remember that God's ways are not our ways.

Mother: That's true. He did a lot of strange things in Old Testament times, like plagues and fiery serpents to punish His Chosen People—and slaying all of this nation or that nation (gasp or realization) even the babies! I forgot about the babies!

Man 2: There, see? That there's the reason I never could see going to church. What kind of God is that—to kill even babies?

Mother: It's not fair! Why should He punish her too? It's not fair!

Man 2: No Ma'am. It's not fair. Or maybe He just doesn't care.

Mother: I'd rather think that of Him—that He doesn't see, or care, rather than that He'd punish us all with death for who knows what transgression. There are so many things that displease Him. I could never keep them all straight. I had to watch every deed, every word, every thought even. It was impossible. How could I think of all that all the time? It was hard enough as a girl, but when I got married to my Jim. And then we had Jessica here. I couldn't be forever going to church when I had a family to take care of. I couldn't sit around praying and reading my Bible when there were clothes to wash and dishes to do. What did He expect, for heaven's sake? (notices that she's being more or less ignored and comes back to the present situation) So we're just going to die here because I, for one, did not go to church enough or read my Bible enough, or pray or or...

Man 1: Take it easy, Ma'am. God is not punishing us. We were warned about taking off like this too late in the year, none of us seasoned travelers. The experts told us about the snow. We just thought we knew better. That's the way we are with God, too.

Mother: Well, what about "All things work together for good"? What good is this?

Man 1: If it brings you closer to God, isn't that good? To my way of thinking, that's the best kind of good. I've had lots of time to think while we're stuck here in the snow. I've seen a lot of things about myself. And I've been finding I'm not too busy any more to read that Bible and pray. I see a lot of things I've been doing wrong—not outside like murder or stealing, but inside—arrogance, pride, faith in my talents and abilities. I was so caught up in my own plans that I didn't bother to ask God whether they were His will, or even if they were a good idea. And when the experts advised against this trip, I thought they just didn't recognize my ability to rise above any adversities.

Mother: You were a fool.

Man 1: We were foolish to think we were smarter than the experts. And it's stupid to think we're wiser than God.

Mother: Well, the Bible says God takes care of fools and children, but the evidence shows that He really doesn't care at all.

Man 1: You're wrong, Ma'am. He sees us.

Mother: (sarcastically) Watching to see how graciously we die?

You're wrong! He doesn't see! He doesn't care! If He cared, would He have let my Jim die in that senseless accident on the road? No! He doesn't care! We're all going to die! We're going to die cold and hungry and alone, just like poor old Mr. Cornwall last night. (slowly raises her head, an idea coming into focus) Mr. Cornwall...Um, I know where we can get some food,

Man 1: You do?

Mother: but I'll need some help getting it.

Man 2: Where?

Mother: Mr. Cornwall's tent.

Man 1: Mr. Cornwall? What did he have?

Mother: (slyly) Well, you never know what he could have kept in there, under cover.

Man 1: I've known Mr. Cornwall for years. I can't believe he would hold out on us. I was with him when he died. If he had food somewhere, why didn't he eat it? He was nothing but bones. I can't believe he'd hoard...(stops and looks at Mother's face. She looks strange. Horror dawns on him and he takes a step away.) No! You're not suggesting...

Mother: Why not? It isn't so awful. We ate the mules, didn't we? We gnawed the leather? What's the difference? Meat is meat. Bone is bone. (getting desperate) We could make soup. Nobody would have to know where we got it. We could say we found something in the woods that died.

Man 1: No! Please, no! We have hides. We can still eat hides...

Mother: I'm tired of hides! I'm not having any more! What do you think I am, an animal? (defensively turning to Man 2) You! What do you think? You said God helps those who help themselves! We've got to provide for ourselves!

Man 2: (horrified) Lady, that's not what I meant. There is common decency...

Mother: (explosively, standing to her feet) Where is common decency? Gone with the God who left us forsaken in the snow. Gone with all the etiquette and nice little sandwiches and tea on Sunday afternoons with Pastor James and Sarah. Gone with prayers that never quite got answered, with Bible promises that didn't mean what they said. Gone with the hopes and dreams for a new life in a new land with my beloved Jim laid in a grave two hundred miles back—our only child nothing left but a wisp of breath. (pleading) What difference will it make? We're going to die anyway. No one will ever even know where to start to look to find us. What use is common decency? Or God?

Man 1: Wait a second here! Is it God's fault we're in this mess? I don't remember Him forcing any of us to get into these wagons.

Mother: But why doesn't He do anything?

Man 1: (quietly) He already has. Whether we die kicking and screaming or in quiet faith will not change the fact that we will die, if not now, then someday. Are you going to accuse Him of being unfair because we die? Jesus paid a terrible price so death would not be the end for us.

Mother: (long silence, then weakly) I'm sorry. It's just that…when I looked into my daughter's face…when I thought of my Jim…It seemed so…unfair.

SCENE II: Man 1 stands with a shovel in hand. Man 2, Mother and Child stand as if by the side of a new grave.

Man 1: Heavenly Father, we commit Robert Cornwall into Your loving hands. We know that he is now with Jesus—as we who remain may well be soon. It is not an easy thing, Lord, to die alone on this mountain, but, though no one else sees, we know You do. You said You would supply all our needs according to Your riches in glory by Christ Jesus. Whether You choose to give us manna, or whether You do not, You still have already supplied our greatest need—that when we die, we will ever be with You. Precious in the sight of the Lord is the death of His saints. Blessed be the name of the Lord. Amen… Amen.

(All freeze. Narrator walks on stage in front of them and addresses the audience.)

Narrator: Members of the Donner Party could have chosen to die with dignity, trusting their souls into the hands of their faithful Creator. Instead, they devoured their dead and became, not an anonymous band of travelers starving on a mountain, but a watchword forever synonymous with the depths of depravity to which human beings might sink if conditions seem desperate enough and they think no one will know.

- The End -

You Never Know...

When people were questioned about their reactions to the story of the Donner Party, they expressed the concern that they might, in similar circumstances indeed do the same thing. Often they cautioned, "Don't ever say you'll never do something because you never know what you'll do until it happens to you." So the fear lurks in the backs of their minds that, under conditions of intense suffering, they might also eat their friend.

I don't believe it's true that you never know what you'll do, implying some dark, spiritual monster that will rear up if you're miserable enough. God has put eternity in our hearts and written right and wrong on them. There is an internal moral compass built into each human being, and I believe in the power of Holy Spirit to keep us aligned with His best for us always. .

Other Choices

If all your students hear about are the gristly failures of humans under duress, and if they're exposed to the Survival of the Fittest logic of a world where they are told they are just another phylum of animal and there's no divine purpose for their lives, they can suffer an underlying worry that, under the right circumstances, their own faith is most likely to fail. But there are many other examples of those who did not sink into insanity or depravity, and it's very helpful for your students to see those accounts. One of them is from within the Donner Party itself.

Virginia Reed was nine years old at the time of the terrible winter. She wrote that every member of her family survived, including all four of the children. Her little sister Patty actually used her doll to entertain the adults in the group. I think she was seven at the time. Can you imagine a child doing her best to lift the spirits of the adults around her? It shows what someone with a sturdy spirit can do, even if she's a very young person.

Virginia wrote that they did not eat human flesh, but, according to her diary, hers was the only family that didn't. She said leather was still available the whole time, but the rest of the party had chosen not to eat it.

Interestingly, Virginia's father, James Reed, was forced to leave the group after he killed a man who would not stop beating an ox. Reed was sent away on horseback. He made it through safely and was able to get help that led to the rescue of the beleaguered survivors. If he had not been sent away, it's doubtful that anyone would have gone looking for the Donner Party and all would have perished in the cold. So some lived on with their memories, which actually might have been worse.

I wrote the following poem after watching a chilling documentary on the Donner Party and reading diaries of people who were there. It was so horrific that most of them never spoke of it at all.

THE DONNER PARTY
a poem

> *They say there's no way you can know what you'll do*
> *When snow piles high and you can't get through,*
> *But I'd rather die with my belly aquiver*
> *Then fight for a bite of somebody's liver.*

The Endurance

In 1914, Ernest Shackleton took 28 men on a trans-arctic expedition aspiring to become the first humans to cross Antarctica. When their ship, The Endurance, became frozen in ice, Shackleton changed his goal from fame to getting everyone safely home. It was sixteen months under horrific conditions, but, through Shackleton's divinely inspired and strong character, good leadership, and supernatural help, all survived, did not succumb to insanity, and nobody got eaten.

In the last desperate attempt to reach help, Shackleton and a few other men took a small boat and managed to get from Elephant

Island to South Georgia, where Stromness Bay whaling station, the only inhabited place in the arctic, was located.

By the time they arrived, only two of the men were deemed strong enough to attempt the climb over the mountains to the station, which was on the other side of the island. With no climbing gear, maps or assurance they would even come out in the right place to find the station, Shackleton and the two men climbed thirty-two hours over the icy, treacherous rocks until, at last, they stumbled to the door of the station. Later Shackleton would comment that he sensed the presence of a fourth man climbing with them in the dark, something another of the men also confirmed. Who was the fourth man?

Choices, Choices, Choices

History, whether biblical or world events, is made of choices. We can see consequences displayed over a span of time. We can feel how they effect us—with a shudder or with a strengthening of heart.

The Donner Party and The Endurance have elements of suffering in common, most obviously the extreme cold and starvation. Yet how different the consequences!

May your students be inspired and encouraged as they see ordinary humans in great difficulties making choices that reveal what can happen when someone trusts the Lord. God can do exceedingly abundantly beyond what we can ask or think—even to the supernatural.

"The LORD is my strength and my shield; My heart trusted in Him, and I am helped; Therefore my heart greatly rejoices, And with my song I will praise Him."
Psalms 28:7 NKJV

Suggestions for Reversal Scripts

—Jacob and Esau (Genesis 25:30)

Esau could have refused to sell and treasured his birthright instead of despising it

—Esau and Isaac (Genesis 27:4)

When Isaac told Esau to get him game and he would bless him, Esau could have admitted that he sold his birthright to his younger brother

—Jacob and Rebekah (Genesis 27:6)

Rebekah could have told Jacob God had given him the birthright and trusted God to give her son favor and blessing from Isaac without the lie and the fake hairy arms and neck coverings.

It helps me to remember that Abraham, Isaac, and Jacob—the fathers of God's chosen nation— all had their problems. They showed undisguised favoritism that caused intense jealousy and strife among the children, they lied. They cheated. They took matters into their own hands and tried to manipulate circumstances to make things come out favorably for themselves, even after God had given them promises, many of which were unconditional. And still they didn't trust Him. Still they didn't obey. Still they faltered and walked heartily after the flesh and not after the Spirit.

It helps me because God was still able to build a remarkable nation from former idolators and slaves, and is continuing the refining work that will make them a shining example of what can happen to a people whose God is the Lord. The fulfillment of their destiny is still yet to come, but we can take comfort in knowing our God does not change, and no matter how much we mess up, we're still engraved on the palms of His hands and He Who began a good work in us is faithful to complete it.

—Saul at Gilgal (1 Samuel 13:11)

With the army scattering away from him and the enemy outnumbering him, he could have continued to wait for Samuel, saying, "If everybody leaves and the enemy increase as the sands of the sea, Lord God, I will trust Thee!"

—The rich young ruler (Mark 10:21)

He could have sold all and followed

—Pilate (John 19;4)
He could have freed Jesus

—Adam and Eve (Genesis 3)
She could have refused to eat the fruit, or she could have been deceived, but Adam still could have remained obedient and interceded for Eve.

—Balaam and his donkey (Numbers 22:25)
When she spoke, he might have listened. Or when she turned away the second time, he could have dismounted and asked the Lord what was wrong.

—Judas and Jesus (John 13:37)
When Jesus sat him in the place of honor and then honored him by giving him the first morsel at the Passover feast, Judas could have recognized the honor and decided to follow Jesus. It's important to recognize that Judas was not set up, predestined to betray the Savior. He had total free will. God, being outside of time, saw what Judas did and inspired Isaiah and others to write the descriptions in their prophecies. Any one of the disciples could have betrayed Jesus. You can see that by their reaction when He told them one of them would. They all wondered if they were the one.

—Peter and the servant girl (Matthew 26;69)
He could have stopped at the second denial, rethought what he was doing, and repented. He could have prepared to be arrested, tortured and killed himself, and discovered that he was allowed to go free. Jesus had said He had lost none of those His Father had given Him, and He would have been able to preserve Peter's life for the calling he had ahead of him.

Into Their Skin
(both now and then)
Writing Biblical Monologues

Wouldn't it be exciting to be able to sit and listen to John the Beloved tell about the Last Supper? Seated in the shadows with the other prisoners on Patmos, we would listen breathlessly as he described his feelings at that unusual Passover. What would he say? Would he tell us how he felt when he heard Jesus talk of going away, of suffering, of even being killed? When Jesus declared that His betrayer was there, what self-doubts crossed John's heart as he leaned against his Master's chest?

The Bible is not only a revelation of God's love, will, and instructions for us, it is also an historical account of the lives of many human beings—people like ourselves who faced problems, struggled with themselves, doubted, feared, and encountered God.

A monologue (a speech by one speaker) is an effective way of helping us understand how people in biblical times related to their problems and to their Savior.

Writing Monologues with a Biblical Perspective

There are a number of ways to handle biblical monologues. One of the simplest is as follows:

1. Choose the biblical individual with whom you most identify.

2. Research that individual, finding every incident relating to the person that's recorded. A concordance is helpful.

3. Select one specific moment, usually some type of crisis in the life of the person. That event becomes the central incident in the monologue.

4. Write the monologue as if you are talking to friends many years after the incident occurred.

Here is an example, a monologue written by my son, Thomas.

Thomas

by Thomas Ramirez

Age: 16 years

I had only known Him for three short years when He was taken away. I'd seen Him open blind eyes, make the lame walk, cleanse lepers, and even raise the dead. I could never figure out just exactly why the Pharisees hated Him so much. All I ever saw Him do was good things for the glory of God. Often, He would stay up all night praying after preaching all day just so that He could do the same thing all over again in the morning.

He was always giving of Himself—whether it was healing and feeding people, or just showing them the way to the Father. He never did it for His own glory. From what John said, even while He was on the cross, He forgave those who tortured Him.

But then, on that cross, He died. Sure we knew the prophesies, but it never seemed to be real, it always seemed so distant.

I felt like a traitor. After all He'd shown me, after all He'd done, I ran away and hid when He needed me most. Sure Peter denied Him, but I wasn't even there. I seemed to remember that He'd said something about coming back to life in three days, but on the third day, nothing special came to me. I didn't see Him walk across the water to greet me, or show up at my house wanting to fellowship. All my hopes just crumbled around me.

A few days later, some of the disciples decided to have a meeting. I chose not to go because I figured that there was no use in it. He was dead. I had learned to deal with that and they would have to also.

After the meeting, they came to me and told me that Jesus had been there. At first, I was glad, but then I remembered that Jesus Himself had warned about false reports in the last days. Maybe the Romans, or even the Pharisees had paid them off to trap me. Sure they were my close friends, but so was Judas.

Not knowing if I should believe them or not, I told them I would not believe until I put my fingers in His palms and my hands in His side. I wasn't even going to show up next time they met, but I couldn't help hoping…wishing that He could really be alive.

The night finally came and all eleven of us were there. Fearing the

Romans, we bolted all the doors and windows, as if that could really stop them.

We hadn't been there very long when we heard a sound like a rushing wind. We all ran to the window and started to unbar it when I heard a voice behind me…it was Jesus.

All doubt fled away as I put my fingers in His palm and my hands in His side.

I guess I didn't really want to believe at first lest I be mistaken and seem like a fool. In spite of all He tried to teach me in the time He was here, I still hadn't learned to trust Him.

I praise God that He is more than willing to show His lost sheep the way for it was then that I trusted the Lord so much that I would follow Him no matter who tried to stop me even if I followed Him to the cross.

Evaluation

For the most part, this monologue is not a reenactment of Thomas's famous first encounter with the risen Christ. Because Thomas was speaking from a perspective of many elapsed years, he could briefly sketch in background information—Jesus' activities, His habits, His character, Thomas's own attitudes and fears after the crucifixion, the moment of facing Jesus. Then he related what the crisis meant to him.

Insight came to my son, as he considered what might have been the reasons for the actions of the disciple: fear—of the Romans, of his "friends," of false Christs, of being a fool. He also recognized that Jesus did not scold Thomas for his lack of faith. Rather, the Lord patiently provided the very proof that Thomas declared he must have, an act of love and understanding which spurred the disciple's life into joyful commitment no matter the cost.

Problems with Endings

The main problem with this monologue is that the whole thing comes to a rather abrupt halt, beginning with the words "All doubt fled away." It's the ending-in-twenty-five-words-or-less syndrome—one of those temptations common to man.

This is perhaps the most crucial place in the monologue. Here, spiritual insight is required. This is also the place where most monologues fail. Students seem to be patient and careful about developing the character and the story line until it reaches the climax. The climax is usually weak, and it's down hill thereafter. Why?

One possible reason is that young people simply haven't had much experience looking back on traumas and processing them out in the Spirit. During their teen years, they may find self-examination extremely painful, especially when dealing with apparent personal failure. This is why it's so beneficial for them to put themselves in the place of biblical people. When they see how Thomas struggled (and failed), when they sense Christ's graciousness to him even as he doubted, when they share the victory of Thomas's resolve to follow, they can receive an infusion of faith and encouragement.

Thomas didn't die from his lack of faith. In fact, Jesus cared so much for Thomas that He made a special effort to build his faith. Jesus understood him, and the acceptance He extended to Thomas invited him to share with his Savior a richer, more trusting relationship, one based on unconditional love rather than human performance.

Another weakness in the script came about because my son's character failed to maintain the proper time frame. His narration degenerated into a retelling of the action rather than remaining a contemplation of a very distant occurrence.

Perhaps it would have helped him to picture his character in jail, sharing his story with other prisoners. In an effort to strengthen their faith in the face of possible martyrdom, the apostle might have wanted to emphasize the truth of Jesus' divinity by detailing the care that Jesus exercised in proving Himself to him (In John 20:25, Thomas declares, "Except I shall see in his hands the print of the nails, and put my finger into the print of the nails, and thrust my hand into his side, I will not believe." Notice, in v. 27, that Jesus says, "Reach hither thy finger and behold my hands; and reach hither thy hand, and thrust it into my side."). That would give the narration a direction and purpose, and might help the writer orient the character's point of view towards a specific goal.

Here are some sample lines:

"I want you all to understand that this Jesus for whom you might be giving your lives is real. I know! I touched Him after His resurrection. At the time of my greatest failure of faith, He made sure I knew the reality of His being alive again. Torture, death, and three days in a tomb were not the end of the story. He rose again as He told us He would. And now, at a time when you might be losing your lives, He wants you to have that same assurance that He is the Resurrection and the Life, and you shall be with Him forever more.

"I said I had to see the print of the nails in his hands—put my finger in them, even—and thrust my hand into His side. Can you imagine how I felt when, only eight days later, suddenly He was there? He beckoned to me, drawing my trembling finger towards the terrible holes, my hand to the awful gash. He told me, 'See! Come look at the nail prints. Touch! Thrust your hand into My side!'

"I didn't want to look, but I couldn't bear not to. How it hurt! He had used the very words I had spoken so few days before. I opened my eyes just a little. I was surprised! Instead of ragged flesh, I saw what appeared to be very old scars! I looked quickly up into His face. He was smiling! I stared again at the scars. He was whole! He was real! I felt my own torn faith smooth and heal as I ran my finger over the tight, smooth skin."

Later, Thomas could say something about the mysterious comment about not seeing, yet believing. He could recall that, at the point of his greatest vulnerability, Jesus met him with tangible proof, but later, he was able to believe without proof because of his faith in the reality and character of the unseen One who always met him at his level and invited him further.

"Now, of course, I understand. He was like that: He'd say something totally bewildering, trusting that, as the Holy Spirit orchestrated aspects of our lives, we would experience, and then understand, the meaning of His statements."

Such lines as, "He was like that," give the listener a sense that the speaker has been in association with the other individual enough that he recognizes patterns of behavior-- aspects of character--that one in a less intimate relationship would not observe.

More Variations

Since Thomas is not limited to his own story or to the chronological retelling of his crisis event, he can recall what later happened to one of his friends—further evidence of Jesus' loving concern for His disciples. Thomas might say, "After that, Jesus did many other signs (John 20:30), but one particularly I remember. It was by the Sea of Tiberius. We had been fishing all night."

Thomas could tell what happened to Peter, showing how Jesus brought him comfort, healing, and restoration in a way specially fitted to address the failure of one who had vehemently denied Him three times.

Whereas Thomas might emphasize the proof of the resurrected Christ to prisoners awaiting death, he would present his story differently if his goal was to help his listeners realize Jesus' concern for each individual and His careful workings to encourage and restore them at their points of failure.

In the following suggested narration, the speaker wrestles with his "sound judgment." In a context of doubt (intellect) and fear (emotions), he recounts a time of near paralysis in his life when all that he trusted to be true had appeared to be broken and brutally murdered—a time of faithlessness without hope. To add to the sense of dialogue with his unseen companions, the narrator asks and answers questions.

"How did I feel? How would you feel if you had just spent three and a half years following a man who looked every bit to you like the real Messiah, only to find Him hanging grotesquely on a Roman cross? Would fear and grief penetrate every moment of your life? What would you say to your heart in the dark? And when the others with faces alight told you He'd suddenly appeared in their midst past all locked doors, would you be anxious to abandon all and believe again?

"I was in anguish—discouraged, disheartened, severely questioning my own sanity, let alone my sound judgment. Was I that gullible to follow Him? If He appeared, would I follow Him again?

"How would you feel if He were suddenly there? Remember, it had been more than a week since they told me they'd seen Him. We'd met every day and nothing had happened. Every day I went through it—doubt, then hope. Doubt. Hope. Doubt..."

Translating into Humanity

Students need guidance in learning how to translate the actions of biblical persons into the realm of every day experience. Once they learn to perceive the humanity in biblical persons, once they understand that the disciples, for example, were just ordinary people who sometimes made humiliating mistakes, once they see that these errors and failures are part of the process of growing, maturing, and learning to rely, not on themselves, but on God, they might begin to recognize that they are not alone in their struggles. Perhaps they will better understand their value, their potential in faith. This writing assignment helps them remember that God still uses foolish things, and with infinite wisdom and care, transforms them into men and women in the image of Christ.

Monologues with Contemporary Expression

Using Twentieth Century terms, monologues with contemporary expression present biblical characters in a more colloquial way. This automatically introduces humor into the accounts because it seems funny to think of biblical people with such concerns as microwaves and Bingo. It also makes it easier for us to relate to them as we place them in surroundings familiar to ourselves.

Be careful, though. While this contemporary element can be fun, care must be exercised to make sure that the writing does not become disrespectful or blasphemous. Teach your students always to be sensitive to the sacred. God must never be mocked. People must never be belittled, cheapened, or devalued. Rather, humor is achieved by incongruity, anachronism, and by the universality of our human experience. And please, please guide your student away from overuse of slang! So easily, so quickly these scripts can get giddy or tedious.

Lot's Wife
by Carolyn Wing Greenlee

SCENE: Lot's Wife stands frozen in a running position with her head turned to look over her shoulder. She slowly relaxes and faces the audience, speaking cordially.

You know, there were some archaeologists here last week—poking around, taking samples, muttering and speculating and wondering. They told the reporters that they were trying to verify the "biblical account of Lot's Wife's being turned into a pillar of salt," but it sounded more to me like they were trying to DIS-prove it. They seemed to have some personal reason for wanting to show that the Bible wasn't historically accurate, and, by the way, that God doesn't mean what He says, or writes, as the case may be.

So they scraped out a little here (She points to her skirt.) and here (She points to her elbow.) and here (She points to the back of her head.) and what did they find? Salt! But did they believe it was really me? No. "So it's an   unusual salt formation," they said, "So what?" (vehemently) So what! I wanted to scream, "It's ME! It's ME! It's ME!" I've been stuck here for who knows how long with nobody to talk to and nothing to do but look back to where I used to live. (wistfully, regretfully) But it's been gone a long, long time.

(resolutely) Well, I've no room to complain. It isn't like I wasn't warned. The angel told me, "Don't look back. " Lot said, "Don't look back." I don't know why I did. I guess, in a moment of stress… There was all the noise, like exploding. I was curious. And maybe I just didn't believe it was really that serious. After all, they just said, "Don't look back." They didn't say why.

Maybe I was just tired. It had been a hard night—all our neighbors yowling around outside like a bunch of tom cats. Now, you've got to understand, they're not a bad sort. Sure, they get a little rowdy sometimes, especially when they've had a bit much to drink, but doesn't everybody? You've got to get to know them, that's all. Live and let live.

So I was tired. And Lot had been really acting strange. He was nervous and kind of twitchy—kept peeking out the windows and pacing around. Those men didn't help either. There was something strange about them, that's for sure. I couldn't put my finger on it, but they were…I don't know…kind of…eerie, like from some other planet or something. Anyway, they made me feel a little creepy.

Lot wasn't helping. He went and told our sons-in-law (nice, decent chaps, mind you) that the LORD was going to destroy the city! He said they had to get out right away! Well, they just laughed. They thought he was joking. It was the middle of the night, for heaven's sake. Be reasonable. It would take at least a day to pack. And why should they leave anyway? Gordy just got a new job, an expense account, and a silver Corvette. Sodom was their home. They liked living there. It wasn't perfect, but no place ever is. They said they were staying. They'd take their chances.

So then, when it got towards dawn, the strange men got stranger still, and started pestering Lot. They told him to take me and the girls and get out! Well, by then, even Lot was wondering if it wasn't just a bad dream. I thought he was coming to his senses. Then they grabbed our hands and dragged us—literally dragged us, mind you, out of the house and down the street, past Marge and Jim's where we play cards every Wednesday night, past the Bingo parlor and our favorite little bar and grill, past the hairdresser where I always got the latest town news, down past the house of my little sister, Jill, and outside the gates. (She starts to breathe hard, as if she has been running.)

Then all I remember was running, running, running. (She begins to act this out as if she's actually fleeing.) I can hear the explosions— huge booming like giant thunder. I smell smoke. The sky is on fire! My lungs are on fire! I'm running! running! I can't breathe! I can't run anymore! I hear screaming! It sounds like Marge! It sounds like Jill! My sister! My friends! My cozy little house! I just can't leave! It isn't fair! What's so horrible about Sodom? What kind of God would kill all those nice people?

Lot has me by the wrist. It hurts. I wrench away. He is running!

running! Huffing and puffing and gasping, "Don't look back!" But wait a minute! What about what I want? Has anybody even bothered to ask me? What about my petunias? Who's going to water my petunias? One more huge boom, a blast of heat, more screams! My friends! "Don't look back!" Another explosion! My petunias! "Don't look back!" It isn't fair! It isn't fair! "Don't look back!" But I must…(She turns her head and freezes mid-sentence.)

(She relaxes again and addresses the audience.) Well, that's what happened. Now you know the whole story. I never dreamed it would turn out this way—one look backward. (She pauses and reflects for a moment.) Actually…I guess…it was a lot of looks backward…or maybe just not enough looking forward. We were just going along in our lives—eating and drinking, buying and selling, planting and building. I had life just the way I liked it—comfortable, easy, pleasant. I didn't want to lose it. But, on the day that Lot went out from Sodom, it rained fire and brimstone from heaven and destroyed it all. I would not listen to the angels— (ruefully) now I know they were angels—because I never learned to listen to God. I was too caught up in the cares of this life. I had no interest in the things unseen—eternal things. I just wanted to keep my life the way I wanted it…so I lost it.

(drawing herself up straight, with resignation and a deep sigh) So, when God calls you out and you find it hard to let go, if you want to haul your stereo or your microwave or your favorite cat with you as you run—if you think you've gotta bury your father or try out your new computer or kiss your sweetie just one last time—if you're out in the field with your hand to the plow and you're tempted to look back—remember Lot's Wife (Slowly she returns to the original frozen position.).

Evaluation

The issue of the Lot's Wife monologue is: Whom shall I serve? Shall I trust God to satisfy me, or shall I continue to want what I want when I want it? Will I trust God's wisdom, or will I try to preserve my life the way that seems right to me?

Modern day arguments and excuses are woven into this monologue ("What kind of God would kill all those nice people?") as well as Scripture ("...on the day that Lot went out from Sodom, it rained fire and brimstone from heaven and destroyed it all."). Both add to the impact of the message.

Tone and Diction

Part of characterization is deciding how the character will see his world. Is it optimistic? Cynical? Is the character aggressive? Some people have an attack-mode approach to life. Tone is the element of writing which shows a certain attitude on the part of the speaker. The events the character chooses to relate and the way he relates them color the facts with his unique point of view.

Diction is choice of words--a manner of expression in words. Every word a character speaks should accurately reflect the world view, the education, the attitudes, and the culture and time period from which that character comes. If a contemporary version of Lot's wife began to speak King James English, that would be an inconsistency in diction. If she were set in Georgia (as were the characters in "The Cotton Patch Gospel"), she would need the idioms (dialect of a people, region, class, etc.), inflections, place names, and cultural institutions of her time.

At best, characters' words will be so consistent that they will not call attention to themselves, but be believable expressions and revelations of their individual personality.

Stage Directions

Stage directions provide additional information about the character. Notice that full sentences follow normal sentence format--a capital at the beginning of the first word and punctuation at the end. Brief directions which are not complete sentences are italicized without those things. Both types of directions are enclosed in parentheses to help the reader recognize that these words are not part of the script.

The Old Issue of My Will Be Done

Especially at Christmas time, we may find ourselves thinking kind thoughts of Mary. How blessed she was to be the mother of Messiah Jesus! But what was it really like for her to live through her unique position in history? When Gabriel brought her news from the throne, here are some questions she could have asked.

"But, what about my reputation?"

"How long will it take?"

"Is it going to hurt?"

"What will Joseph think?"

"How will I ever explain this to my mother?"

There are many questions Mary could have asked, but Scripture records just one--a very reasonable one--"How can this be, seeing I know not a man?"

It is valuable to discuss the mores and morals of the times. What was the penalty for pregnancy before marriage? What exactly did Mary face as she accepted the will of God? Considering the cost and the conclusion, was it worth the sacrifice? It was going to be much more grueling than Mary could imagine. Perhaps that's why Gabriel started out with assurance of her favor with God and His blessing upon her.

After accepting the call, there were other things to process. Being a good Jewish girl, Mary knew the Scriptures. She must have known Isaiah 53. She also must have wondered how she would manage such an enormous responsibility as mothering the Messiah. In the following monologue, the audience can ponder these questions with Mary as she considers them with the tiny King in her arms.

Mary's Monologue
from "Yet Another Christmas Play"
by Carolyn Wing Greenlee

(Mary mimes holding baby Jesus. She speaks to Him fondly). You're such a good baby! I was so worried—the long, bumpy ride, and then no room anywhere for us to stay. (looks around) It isn't exactly what I had in mind, but then, since the angel came, nothing has been anything like what I had in mind. Papa always taught me that we could never guess what Adonai would do, but, whatever

He did, we could be sure it was right and just, because He is always good. So why should I expect anything else?

(looking apprehensive) Sometimes I'm reminded of the prophecies—how You must suffer for the sins of Your people—and I'm frightened for You. (taking courage and speaking bravely) But it only means that I must learn to trust Adonai even more. You are God's little Lamb. He will take care of You. So just close Your eyes now and go to sleep. He Who set the stars in place is watching over You. And somehow, when I'm holding You, I feel Him holding me.

Monologues with a Long-Range Perspective

We live in the day of the instantaneous. Push the button. Flick the switch. We tend to be impatient, impulsive, imprudent—living as if there were no tomorrow. Our students at fourteen, fifteen, sixteen years old have little sense of the long-range—either of possibilities or of consequences. This writing exercise addresses that problem.

When the builders laid the foundation of the temple of the LORD, the priests stood in their apparel with trumpets, and the Levites, the sons of Asaph, with cymbals, to praise the LORD according to the ordnance of David King of Israel. And they sang responsively, praising and giving thanks to the LORD:

"For He is good, for His mercy endures forever toward Israel."

Then all the people shouted with a great shout, when they praised the LORD because the foundation of the house of the LORD was laid. But many of the priests and Levites and heads of the fathers' houses, who were old men, who had seen the first temple, wept with a loud voice when the foundation of this temple was laid before their eyes; yet many shouted aloud for joy, so that the people could not discern the noise of the shout of joy from the noise of the weeping of the people, for the people shouted with a loud shout, and the sound was heard afar off." Ezra 3:10-13

After seventy years of captivity, the children of Israel were allowed to return to their land. The temple which had been so shockingly devastated was being rebuilt. At the site were those who were born in captivity—those who had never known anything but Babylon. Also standing with them were "many of the priests and Levites and heads of the fathers' houses, who were old men, who had seen the first temple." They did not shout. Scripture reports that they "wept with a loud voice." It is from the perspective of these old ones that this long-range monologue was written.

Elimelech Bar-Aaron
by Thomas Ramirez
age: 16 years
(Ezra 3:12)

(prophetic-sounding voice) And this whole land shall be a desolation and an astonishment, and these nations shall serve the king of Babylon seventy years. Then it will come to pass, when seventy years are completed, that I will punish the king of Babylon and that nation, the land of the Chaldeans.

(old man voice) Seventy years...seventy years of memories. Waking up every morning ready to take my place in Solomon's temple, but knowing the grim reality of its destruction. Seventy years of mental anguish remembering the gilded doors, the bronze sea, the golden shields. All carried off to Babylon. Carried into captivity. I can still remember the cry of anguish of my people as we were torn from the arms of our tearful loved ones and dragged away from the city. The urgent prayers to Adonai for protection. The acrid smoke of burning buildings. The once beautiful city...a burnt heap of rubble.

Jerusalem, Jerusalem. We would have defended you had God not turned away. Throughout our bondage, many of us stayed faithful, and now our God has given us His favor once again and you are the fruit of our effort. Yes, God is once again among us and you are rebuilt. It is as if it were only yesterday that those horrors were done in you, but it must have been long ago. So long ago... (He looks down at his feet. When he looks up, he is a young man.)

God, this isn't fair. I am of the priestly line of Aaron. Why isn't my name on the list of the king's personal slaves? I should at least have that position. I am as deserving as Daniel. What does he have that I haven't got? And, God, he's a show off. He had to get special attention even among his brethren. He had to make a big fuss over the food. At least I would have been dignified about it. I wouldn't have merely requested water and vegetables, I would have demanded it as my right as a slave...If I had any. (Looks down at his feet. When he looks up, he is old again.)

Father, I repented of my pride. My attitude was much better after that. The shock of being dragged away from priesthood and prestige to slavery and disgrace...It was too hard for my young mind to handle. I did learn to deal with it, didn't I? (He raises his hands towards heaven and looks up. He is now in his mid 30's.)

God, this situation is not warranted. I deserved the position as a satrap for Darius. Lord, I understand that You kept me from being forced to worship the golden statue of Nebuchadnezzar, but not being a high enough official for that is hardly a good reason. I could have done exactly the same thing that Shadrach, Meshach and Abed-Nego did.

Father, I am glad for what you did to Belshazzar. He deserved death after what he did to our temple goblets and utensils. Why, when I was told to get those so that he could drink out of them, I was incensed. Of course, I did what I was told, but I was only doing what I was told. I knew You needed a good reason to smite him. I was only doing what I thought You would want.

But God, I do think that I deserve some sort of promotion. I can do anything Daniel can do. Oh sure, this is promotion. So I don't dig ditches anymore... I wash dishes. These hands were made to serve in Your temple, or at least rule over the Gentiles...not wash their dishes. (Raises hands towards heaven and looks up. He is old again.)

Lord, I see Your point, I stumbled again. I admit I was wrong there, but it was traumatic to go into captivity without first coming out of another captivity. It is bad to only be a captive of the captives. I was still faithful to pray...most of the time. (Clenches hands together and looks up. He is in his fifties.)

Father, the equity in this situation is doubtful. You have always told us to honor whatever government is over us, yet You blessed Daniel who went totally opposite of what the king decreed. I feel that he should have done what the law stated, but You protected his disobedience while I am still only a lower ruler. Lord, I am grateful that I wasn't a satrap or a governor. The lion's den doesn't have the prestige I deserve. At least, I can continue to work for the position that is rightfully mine.

But God, I still don't understand why You won't bless me. I even married a good Jewish girl...an Aaronite, no less. But do you honor that sacrifice on my part, staying away from the beautiful Gentile women even when my fellow Jews were chasing them? No, You killed her in the disgrace of barrenness. After all I told my friends about how they should be...following You like I do, and You don't even give me a daughter. How could You be so cruel? (Clenches hands together and looks up. He is old again.)

Oh, Father, I see my foolishness. I have despised the blessings and provision and protection that You have given me, thinking only of my own desires. I have defiled the temple of my mind, choosing my own ways rather than Your ways, and trying to do it by following my plan. Surely, I am but dust which has sought to rise up against the living God. Although I remained clean on the outside, on the inside I was filthy and broken down...like the temple has been for seventy years. Torn down, burnt, without even one stone left standing upon another. Lord, let me be like this new temple. I know I will never have the glory You intended for me, but at least, I will be serving You out of love rather than out of duty. I will be doing it Your way instead of mine.

Facing Consequences Without Having To Suffer Them

Young people don't usually think too much beyond their present years. The future seems a long way off. They feel invulnerable, invincible, unaccountable, immortal (while, at the same time, paradoxically feeling helpless and insignificant). This exercise gives them an opportunity to make worldly choices and witness the result.

In this monologue, Elimelech recognizes his accountability when he views the foundation of the new temple, reviews the events of his life, and understands the ramifications of his own choices. Elimelech sees that his sin has not been in his failure to keep the Law, but in attitudes. Rather than trusting God's good intentions for him even in captivity, Elimelech has complained, justified himself, heaped contempt on others less "holy." In the end, however, he recognizes his arrogance and folly.

The wonderful thing about this monologue is that Elimelech understands enough of the heart of God to be able to turn to Him, knowing that he will be received and forgiven. On the other hand, the sentence which begins, "I know I will never have the glory You intended for me, but at least," implies that there is immeasurable, irretrievable loss.

Once again, this concept reflects the legalistic church my sons and I were still attending at the time Thomas wrote this monologue. After we left the church, we had a number of deep and restorative conversations on the nature of God and our relationship with Him. All of us have been able to live the subsequent decades in the love and grace of our Redeemer God. Though we believe a life of judgmental legalism results in years of missing the enjoyment of a gracious God, we also believe Romans 8:28. Even what has been lost can be transformed into good, for Jesus knows how to redeem even that which seems hopelessly destroyed.

Deciding the Character

In preparing to write a monologue with a long range perspective, the student must first decide who his character is. In the case of this exercise on Ezra, a male person can be a priest, a Levite, or a head of house. A female can be a singer in the temple (Ezra 2:65; Neh. 7:67), or a sister, daughter, or wife of any of the above. Students will find it easier to care and write about a character with whom they can identify. The following biblical references provide information about the activities of the various groups of people:

The duties of the Levites are described in I Chronicles 23-25. They were officers and judges, gate-keepers, treasurers, and musicians. Some of these were positions of power and great responsibility. Levites were also assigned to help the priests in their duties.

The priests prepared and presented offering sacrifices and offerings, and ministered before the LORD within the holy place. Only Aaron and his sons could minister directly in the Holy of Holies. Exodus and Leviticus have a wealth of information about the priesthood.

Information about the heads of fathers' houses can be found in I Chronicles 27.

Questions that Help Fill Out Character

Once the students have decided on their character, they must determine the following types of things (you may discover other elements not listed here which are meaningful for your students specifically):

1. What is the physical appearance of the character—height, weight, color of hair, build, etc. What did they look like at the various stages of life?

2. What were they doing when taken into captivity? What were they being trained for? Example: to be a gatekeeper, a singer, or a priest? Before being carried off, how much exposure did they have to the things of God?

3. Where were they when taken? Did they witness the destruction of the temple? What do they remember of former life in Jerusalem?

4. How much understanding did they have of the significance of the temple? Some children have more spiritual perception than others. This will determine what kind of reaction the characters will have when seeing the foundation of the new temple.

5. Did they hear the prophecies of Jeremiah? Did they believe them? Did they remember them in Babylon? When seeing the new foundation, do they remember what Jeremiah said?

6. What happened in Babylon? Did they know about Daniel? Did they hear about Shadrach, Meshach and Abed-Nego? Were they slaves? Did they become respected and receive more responsibility in Babylon? Did they remain pure or compromise? Did they compromise, but later repent and try to live for God in spite of the pagan influence?

7. What happened when they returned to Jerusalem? Did they recognize their sin? Did they regret past choices? Were they glad for their stand for God? Why did they weep—from joy or sorrow?

8. How old were the characters when taken into captivity? This will determine how old they are at the time of the monologue.

9. What are the characters' views of God in the various stages of their lives?

Students may choose not to use all this information in their monologue, but the more "facts" they know about their character, the easier it will be for them to develop a consistent characterization. Item 1, the physical description, is especially helpful in making the character concrete in the students' minds, although those details will probably not appear at all in the writing. Your students need to remember that their characters will be changing ages, and that diction, vocabulary, and actions need to be consistent with those ages.

You might think that these narrow parameters will inhibit the student's flow of ideas. I have found the opposite to be the case: the more specific the assignment, the more free the compositions. Once the student has answered the questions on the list, it is simply a matter of assembling the monologue. It will practically write itself.

Here is an example of some possible elements:
  1. She is a daughter of Asaph training to be a temple singer.
  2. At 14 years old, she witnesses the destruction of the temple, and is carried off to Babylon.
  3. Disillusioned because she has misunderstood God's promises and intentions, she decides to get all she can for herself of protection, provision, and satisfaction.
  4. She compromises in Babylon, becoming a singer for the court of the king.
  5. She marries a Gentile and has a family, choosing not to teach her sons about her God.
  6. Her husband dies, and she returns to Israel. As an old lady of 86, she grieves as she hears the temple singers—realizing what her choices have given her.

Daughter of Asaph
by Carolyn Wing Greenlee
(Ezra 3:12)

SCENE: A woman of 86, slightly bent, stands apart from the crowd at a vantage point overlooking the site of the new temple in Jerusalem. She murmurs to herself—

It seems like a dream—the crowds, the shouts, the healthy young people with their faces all alight...Many were born in Babylon. I wonder if they really understand what they're shouting about...We had to know. Even though I was just a young girl, I'd been training for years. They made sure we understood...(She looks to the side, then up, as if looking intently into the face of her teacher. She is about ten years old.)

(nodding and reciting obediently and eagerly, with a trace of pride) Yes. I understand. As a daughter of Asaph, I am eligible to serve in the temple, but I must wait until I am 29 years old. It is not enough to know by words. Unless I live years of experiencing the mercy, guidance, and lovingkindness of God, I will have nothing in my praise but my own voice. There will be no love, no trust, no true relationship, no worship. I must prepare even now, and be set apart as if by a wall. Only those who have cleansed themselves, those with clean hands and a pure heart, may lift their voices in service in music in the place that the LORD, our God, has chosen to put His Name. Only those who will sanctify themselves may handle the holy things.

(The eager, youthful look fades. The old woman looks down, re-gretfully.). Ah, these young people, so full of life and joy—so eager! Their whole lives stretch ahead of them and they feel invincible! (She leans forward, cupping one ear.) That song! I remember it well! I was learning that song when they came! (She closes her eyes tight-ly, as if drawing the words out of her memory. She sings haltingly at first, then a little more strongly in a quavering voice, then stands more and more erect as she becomes a fourteen year-old girl singing in a training class.)

For H-He is g-good...His His mer - cy endures for... toward Israel. For He is good, for His mercy endures forever towar...(She stops abruptly, with horror on her face..). What's that noise? Who are those men? You can't come in here! Oh, Teacher! Stop them! No! Leave me alone! Let go of me! (She struggles with invisible assailants, then freezes, staring in horror.) No! No! Not the temple! They're taking the gold, the sacred utensils! Oh! LORD God! Stop them! Smite them for this wickedness! (She struggles again, but she cannot get away.) Merciful LORD! Don't let them take me! Oh please! Oh, Great LORD God! Please! (She freezes looking imploringly heavenward, then her face and eyes become old again. She looks very tired and bent.)

(listlessly) He didn't stop them, of course. If I had truly listened to what Jeremiah cried in the streets, I would have understood. But I was very young and so involved in my vocal training and my dreams and my silvery soprano voice…

(She peers to the left, as if not wanting to be caught staring. She is thirteen.) Oooh, Rachel! There he is again! What's he saying? (pause to listen, then a look of impatience) Oh. It's the same old thing he always says, (slightly mocking in a deep voice) "Woe unto him that builds his house by unrighteousness, and his chambers by injustice! Woe unto the shepherds that destroy and scatter!" It's the same old thing he's been saying as long as I can remember. (pause, listening to him) Rachel, do you think he's a real prophet? (pause for answer) I don't know. The other prophets say the exact opposite. Who do you believe? If he's a real prophet, everything he says will come true. He's been talking about God's judgment for years—and has it happened? Maybe he's just a crazy old man.

We're not all as bad as he says. God loves us. He says He's engraved us on the palms of His hands. He says He'll never forget us—never leave us or forsake us. (She pauses as if listening.) Now don't you start in on that. You sound like Jeremiah. Rachel, we've both been in training for years. Don't you think I know all that stuff by now? Do you think for a minute I would risk being able to serve in the Temple? (pause, listening, then in a slightly offended tone) Well, of course I'm keeping myself pure and clean! I obey and honor my father and my mother and I stay far away from the Gentile boys (giggles) no matter how cute they are.

(She returns to her aged state.) I see it now. Even as a girl I had not truly taken to heart the teachings of the wise ones. I knew the words by heart. I could say all the right things. I knew every proper response. I did all the right things. And so I believed I was safe, even in a foreign land.

(She begins preening in a mirror as she talks to Rachel. Now she is twenty.). Just think, Rachel! If we were back in Israel, It would still be nine long years before I could even be considered for service in the temple. And here our teachers say I've done so well that I am ready to sing now. And for the KING, no less. Oh, don't look so sour! I know what I'm doing. I don't mean a word I'm singing, so don't worry! (She listens, then becomes a bit defensive.) No, I haven't forgotten the LORD God. Yes, I remember the Temple. I remember seeing it ravaged and ruined and the holy things carried off like the spoils of war! I remember that nobody seemed to be able to stop any of it. So here we are. We might as well make the best of it. Who knows if we'll ever see Jerusalem again?

(She sighs, aged and bent, looking at the temple site.) Jerusalem. The Holy City. When I was twenty, I never gave a second thought to the time I might some day be old. Though Jeremiah spoke of seventy years of captivity, my mind could not comprehend. The future was nothing but delightful plans. Obviously the God who did not keep us out of captivity had little or no real power in this exciting new land. I began to choose my own way.

(She answers the door, sees her friend, and lights up. She is now thirty-two.) Rachel! I'm so glad to see you! It has been a long time, hasn't it! Yes, yes, we are all well. The boys are growing like weeds! When Tamron has a little extra time, we're going to take them to the country. They really love... (stops abruptly, then resumes, but no longer breezy) Well, no. I haven't told them about HIM (glances heavenward). I saw no need. (listens, then speaks with irritation) Rachel, you haven't changed a bit! Don't you see? Things are different now! Times have changed.

(listens) Okay, you want an example? Take my marriage. What were we always taught? If we even looked at a Gentile boy it would be lightning from the sky. Instantly we'd be cut off from our people! But Tamron and I have been married nearly ten years now and there haven't been any lightning bolts. Not even a rumble of thunder from a distant dark cloud. And we've had a good marriage. Better than most.

So what was I supposed to do, sit around hoping I'd get back to Jerusalem to serve in some temple that would take twenty years to rebuild? And for what? To serve a God that would let us be conquered over and over? Tamron has shown me some things, Rachel.

At first I thought Jeremiah was right, that it was divine judgment. But now I see differently. The scribes and priests had us just where they wanted us—scared to death even to lift a finger on the Sabbath, terrified of "contamination" from the Gentiles, forever bringing this offering or that sacrifice—and it was always the best animals. And who got to eat them? The priests! Don't you see? It was all for control! And Jeremiah had us all so brainwashed from years and years of hammering on us the same old thing, so convinced of our sin and wickedness, that we hardly even resisted when the armies came and carried us off.

But, frankly, I think it was the best thing for us. I could have spent my whole life missing out on all these good things. I would have been stuck away forever contemplating my sin and trying to stay holy, trying to please a God who was never satisfied no matter how hard we tried. My choices haven't hurt me. I think I'm doing quite well for myself. Tamron is well respected and I have three strong sons. If marrying a Gentile is such a horrible sin, why have I been so blessed?

(earnestly) Look, Rachel, you have your life, I have mine. You live according to your convictions and that's fine for you. You choose to teach your sons about God. I choose to let mine make their own choices. There's more than one way to look at things, you know.

(She is old again.) Yes, more than one way to look, but only one way that is right. Two years we have been restored to this land. Two years I have had to review my life. Rachel's sons and daughters have been selected to serve in the temple. They are amongst the singers now. My own sons would not even come to this land with me. Rachel stands with a radiant face, tears of joy flowing from her eyes. She is not ashamed to face the Living God. (hesitates) And I? (long pause)

It has been so many years--so many years I have not believed, so many years I have chosen what I thought was best for me. I did not understand His good intentions towards me—that what He required would ultimately bring me satisfaction, rich fulfillment, (sighs) true peace. Tamron is dead. I am alone. My heart feels dull within me. It is heavy and hard. Though I see the Truth now, the fulfillment of prophecy, the wisdom and power of God's ways, it is difficult to lift my hands. It is difficult to form the words of praise. I am old, and so tired...so tired...

No Christianese Please!

It is important to teach your students not to write "Christianese" endings—where everyone gets saved and lives happily ever after. Notice how the monologue of the daughter of Asaph did not end with her repentance and restoration. Like Esau, her heart had become hardened by years of choices for Self and she was unable to find the place of repentance, even though she recognized her need for a change of heart. It is also important to teach them that getting saved is not the end of the story. After salvation, there are struggles, trials, growth, failures, repentance, restoration, pressing on—running with patience the race set before us, and growing in the wonders of a deep and personal relationship with the Creator of the Universe..

Ending with Hope

I don't personally like things which end with hopelessness (although sometimes that might be the most effective way of getting a message across). While it is true that people really do lose out with God, it is equally true that He is unbelievably patient and long-suffering. Have you ever noticed that the first thing out of winter's bare branches is blossoms? Blossoms for hope. That's straight from the heart of God. Everywhere in creation He signals His power to bring new life. Beauty for ashes.

Young people can become so overwrought with their feelings of failure that they eventually give up. They don't realize that everyone who is serious with God struggles with awareness of their inadequacy to measure up. That's why Grace is such good news. Let us never give them the impression that we are perfect, or that they are too difficult for even Jesus to work with. That's not what He says. Long after our patience--and even our own hope--is exhausted, He continues to pursue, to woo, to draw--all with His remarkable, relentless grace.

A Hopeful Ending

The ending of this monologue could avoid being Christianese and yet convey a sense of hope simply by adding the following words: (looks up slowly, listening, then singing softly, hoarsely) F -F -For He is …good…His mercy endures for…forever…For He is good… (softly) Lord, you said You engraved us on the palms of Your hands and You would never forget us. We are here in Jerusalem once again, though it seemed an impossible dream…(She pauses, thinking, then singing with a little more courage.) Your mercy endures forever…Your mercy endures for…for…(whispers) for me? (closes her eyes and looks hopeful).

At the beginning of the monologue, the character sings those words. As a temple singer in training, she states that she needs to live her faith before she will be ready to serve in the temple. The truth has been planted in her mind, but it gets dislocated by the shock of captivity. Repeating the song at the end brings the monologue full circle--back to the present, but now resounding with the overtones of her experiences and choices. They also leave the door open for her return.

Biblical monologues on Ezra 3 are not limited to accounts of failure and compromise. If all had compromised in Babylon, there would have been none fit to serve in the new temple. Yet, among those born in captivity were singers, gate keepers, priests, Levites— enough for the service of God. A biblical monologue with a long-range perspective can emphasize to young people the blessings and rewards of purity, self-discipline, and responsiveness to Divine Calling. It can also remind them that it's never too late to come home.

Monologues and the Goodness of God

Writing biblical monologues can make us deal first hand with difficult issues in a very personal way. What would it have been like, for example, to be a part of the group which celebrated with David as the Ark crossed the threshing floor, as the oxen stumbled and Uzzah was struck dead? What would a young man have thought as he stood on the hillside, a stone in his hand, knowing that the girl who had caught his eye was being destroyed with her family and all of their possessions because of the sin of her father, Achan?

In our humanness, we might be tempted to charge God with a bad temper, yet the Bible tells us that God is good, consistent, and just. but sometimes it doesn't look that way, both in the Bible (especially the Old Testament) and in history.

Some Thoughts About Ussah

God is not given to tantrums. God is love, and He's good all the time. What loving reason might He have had for the action He took when Ussah touched the ark?

One way to look at this swift judgment is to recognize in it God's severe mercy. What would have happened had God not stricken Uzzah? All of Israel would have known that God doesn't mean what He says. He need not be feared because He did nothing when His strict orders were disregarded. Like willful children, they could have become fairly nonchalant about heeding those orders, not realizing that He was trying to provide for and protect them, and draw them into a secure, safe, and specially blessed place in His Kingdom. Through them, all the nations of the world would be blessed. Messiah would be born as one of them. A holy people was being formed from former pagans and slaves. Through them, God intended to reveal Himself and redeem everything from the devastation of The Fall.

Good from the Fear of the Lord

How do people, by the fear of the Lord, depart from evil? Months after the Children of Israel were safely established in their inheritance on the other side of Jordan, the tribes of Reuben and Gad, and half of the tribe of Manasseh, built an altar in Canaan—not for sacrifice or burnt offering, but as a witness for their children—proof that they had their inheritance with the rest of the tribes though they, themselves, had chosen to live across the river.

Greatly alarmed, a delegation from the other tribes was dispatched to question the purpose of the altar and to kill the wayward ones, if necessary.

This is what they said: "...rebel not against the LORD, nor rebel against us, in building you an altar beside the altar of the LORD our God. Did not Achan the son of Zerah commit a trespass in the accursed thing, and wrath fell on all the congregation of Israel? And that man perished not alone in his iniquity." (Joshua 22;19, 20)

The lesson in the Valley of Achor had been effective. The children of Israel were afraid of God, and they hadn't forgotten what happened to those who were not. They said, "Don't you remember Achan? Do you want to get us all killed?" The judgment on Achan and his family kept the rest of Israel in healthy fear. The stoning was, in actuality, a severe mercy, a loving act.

It is good to remember, too, that death is not the end of the story. There is no certainty that any of Achan's family (or Achan or Uzzah for that matter) went to hell.

Working out Real Life Issues

Solomon said there is nothing new under the sun. Human beings face the same issues century after century. The Bible shows that quite clearly. But it may help students to work through such things as peer pressure or compromise with the world when they are "play acting" in an entirely different environment—such as a harem. If your student wants to perform a monologue she writes for Esther, it might be fun for her to have some props, such as a diaphanous scarf or use a setting where she delivers the lines from a pile of luxurious pillows.

In Harem #2 (Esther 2)

King Ahasuerus (Uh-HAS-you-where-us) was looking for a new queen. All the eligible young maidens had been gathered together and given beauty treatments for a year as they waited in Harem #1 to meet the king. Then, one a day, a maiden was taken to the king. The next morning, she was escorted to Harem #2. Scripture says, "She would not see the king again unless he delighted in her and she was called for by name."

In Ahasuerus' kingdom, young girls were not brought up with the same values as the Hebrews. Hadassah (Esther's Hebrew name) would have to choose how she would present herself, with modesty and purity, or adopting the tactics of the other girls with whom she had spent a year of preparation. They were idolaters, worshiping in ways the God of Israel called abominations.

I wonder what Hadassah pondered in her heart as she waited in Harem #2. No one knew she was Hebrew, so no one expected her to act in accordance with the spiritual and moral laws of the God of the Hebrews. Did she second-guess her behavior, berating herself for being too modest and respectful, not flirty and seductive like other girls? Did she simply trust she had done what the Lord inspired her to do? Did she act in accordance with the ways of God her uncle Mordecai had taught her?

The issue of worth and integrity is something all people face, but it's particularly pressing when they are young and doing their best to find who they are and how to navigate a complex world where rules are always changing and values can be very different from what they were brought up to believe are pleasing to God.

This scene offers opportunity to explore those issues. It can be written as a monologue or as a group piece with others in the harem talking about what they did to gain the favor of the king. It wasn't simply a matter of physical attractiveness; all of them were beautiful. What was it about Hadassah that won her favor with the chief eunuch and then with the king himself? She had something no one else had—the grace and peace of a life surrendered to the Lord, an enduring beauty that shines through those who choose to live trusting in Him, transformed by the renewing of their minds.

Additional Suggestions for Monologues

Genesis 6-9 —Shem, Ham, and Japeth. Three sons of Noah. Three personalities. How did each one of them see the ark project? In 120 years, what might have crossed their minds? In Chapter 10, their offspring are listed. Shem's line produced David and Messiah. Ham's produced Nimrod (who built the wicked cities Nineveh and Babylon), the Canaanites, the Hittites, the Jebusites, the Amorites, the Girgashites, the Hivites, and Casluhim, from whom came the Philistines. (AMP) What does that tell you?

Genesis 16, 17, 21 —Hagar. What changes did she pass through as she first became the mother of a son, ran away, was instructed by the Angel of the Lord to return, went back, and then found herself and her teenaged son thrown out in the desert?

Genesis 21 —Ishmael. He was the pride of his father's life for about fourteen years. Then, suddenly, here was another kid--the Child of Promise, and Ishmael was forgotten. "Now Sarah saw the son of Hagar...mocking Isaac," and the next thing he knew, he and his mother were trudging through the desert without any water. Genesis 16:12 says, "And he will be as a wild ass among men; his hand will be against every man and every man's hand against him." (AMP) How do these things go together?

Genesis 22 —Issac. He was, according to the historian Josephus, perhaps twenty-five years old when he and Abraham climbed Mount Moriah. Easily he could have overpowered his ancient father. But there he was, laying himself down on the altar. Why? What did he expect?

Genesis 39 —Potiphar's wife. What did she think after Joseph fled? Did it cause her to consider her ways? And what about Potiphar himself, for that matter? He was an officer of Pharaoh, the captain and chief executioner of the royal guard. He could easily have had Joseph killed. Why didn't he?

Mark 11:11, 15, 27 —one of the sellers in the temple. He had seen Jesus in the temple before. Was he brought to conviction? Did he change?

Mark 8:22-26 —a blind man. He was told not to even enter the village after he was healed. Was it because Jesus knew the man's friends and relatives would cause him to doubt and, ultimately, lose his healing with their scoffing unbelief? What did he choose to do?

John 1:35-40 —a disciple of John. Two were standing with John. One was Andrew. Who was the other? Did he decide the price of discipleship to Jesus was too high?

John 4:6-30, 39-42 —The Samaritan woman. Like so many today, she was looking for a man to fill the emptiness in her life. Five husbands later, she was still not satisfied. Jesus brought her understanding that no human relationship (no matter how wonderful it might be) could ever quench the thirst or satisfy the heart. How can a student writing this monologue communicate this truth to an audience of people still seeking their fulfillment in relationships with Mr. (or Miss) Right?

Luke 22:54-62 —a certain servant girl. Was she secretly seeking, as did others among the servants of the powerful? Was she disappointed because she wanted to ask more questions, hoping to find the answers to the emptiness of her life?

Luke 24:13-53 —Cleopas on the way to Emmaus. Jesus honored him with a revelation of Himself. What happened to him afterwards?

Luke 24:1-11 —Joanna, wife of Chuza, Herod's chief steward. She was one who traveled with Jesus and supported Him from her own private means. She was there at the cross. She was there at the empty tomb. Did she have to deal with a resentful husband? Was her devotion to God a source of jealousy for him, or did he, too, perceive the reality of Messiah Jesus?

John 14:8; Acts 8:5 —Philip. In his days with Jesus, he didn't seem to be very impressive, but in Acts, just look at him go! What happened to him?

Luke 9:57-61 —three potential disciples. When Jesus challenged them directly, what did they choose?

Mark 15:21 — Alexander and Rufus. What might these brothers have thought when they saw their father bearing the cross for the Christ? In Romans 16:13, Paul refers to Rufus and his mother. Was it the same Rufus? If so, what became of Alexander?

Young People in the Bible

When I was little, there was always the threat of the Red Button. We had drills where the siren would go off and we'd have to get under our desks, crouching on our knees, fingers laced tightly together over the backs of our necks to protect our spines from being severed by glass shattering from the windows. It made me feel very small, helpless, and vulnerable.

People today can also feel small and vulnerable, even after they grow up. But it's much worse when they're young. What can a child do in such a difficult world?

Scripture gives us a number of circumstances in which a child or a young person made a huge difference in a crisis. The most spectacular, of course, is David and Goliath, but there are others who didn't have to face anything nearly as traumatic, yet they, and their actions, mattered.

One is the boy with the five loaves and two fish. A skit expressing his reaction to giving up his food could go any number of directions—from worry about giving up what was his to joyful giving because he was so impressed with Jesus.

And then there is little Samuel himself, serving the Lord as a child, receiving a prophetic word for Eli, the first of many he would be given to deliver in difficult circumstances.

There are numerous possible monologues for young people. Here are some of them.

—Rhoda, the servant girl who heard Peter at the door but didn't believe it was really him so she left him out in the street

—Naaman's servant girl, who suggested he see the Hebrew prophet about a cure for his leprosy

—Paul's nephew, who overheard the plot against his life

—the boy who fetched Jonathan's arrows as David hid. Did he suspect anything?

—Jonathan, who could have been king, but honored God's choice of David over his own advantage

—Mark, who must have wondered if Paul would accept him back into the ministry

—the children the disciples tried to shoo away, saying they were bothering Jesus. How would they feel when Jesus called them to Himself and then said such surprising things about their worth?

—Jairus' daughter back from the dead.

—Eutychus, who fell into a deep sleep as he sat In a window and, as Paul was "long preaching, he fell down from the third loft, and was taken up dead." (Acts 20:9) What a shock! Some have used this story to illustrate the hazards of falling asleep in church, but there are other lessons that can be explored—messages of redemption and new life even when we fall asleep.

—John, the little brother of James. He probably never suspected that he would be an elder in the church and the writer of the most startling revelation of all time.

God's Wisdom in Choosing People

Man looks on the outward appearance. God looks on the heart. (1 Samuel 16:7)

Saul was tall, handsome, kingly. David's brothers were older and stronger than he, and experienced in battle. David was probably sixteen, a shepherd whose only experience with a weapon was a slingshot and stones. When Samuel was sent to anoint one of Jesse's sons to take Saul's place as king, he could not have guessed that God had chosen the teenager who spent his hours of solitude communing with the Lord of the universe.

Ordinary People

Our culture commends the rich, famous, flamboyant, and powerful, but God often uses ordinary people to change history.(2 Samuel 14-17) Sometimes there is no way to get the job done unless you don't seem to be anything special. My favorite example is the serving girl who is sent out from the palace (now occupied by Absalom, the usurper) to take word to two boys—Ahimaaz Zadok's son, and Jonathan Abiathar's son, who are waiting to receive information to deliver to King David who is in hiding. The message will reveal what he must do to escape Absalom's murderous attack. (2 Sam 17:17) If the girl had been gorgeous, high ranking, or more noteworthy in any way, she might not have been able to do that crucial errand.

I wonder what the girl thought, though. She had to be nonchalant and acting normal, drawing no attention to herself, while carrying the message that would save King David's life. If David had been ambushed and killed, Messiah's line would have been broken and there would be no salvation for the world today. Do you think the serving girl knew what she was asked to deliver? If so, it was an enormously heroic deed on her part.

God is not opposed to people having money. Abraham was wealthy, and so was Joseph of Arimathea. He is not opposed to the beautiful. In fact, He creates some with extraordinary comeliness for special reasons. Esther needed that asset to qualify for a position as queen that enabled her to save her people from annihilation. Moses was a beautiful baby that Pharaoh's daughter decided to adopt as her own, though royal orders decreed that all Hebrew baby boys be drowned in the Nile. And there are accounts of brilliant and powerful individuals such as Deborah the judge and Cyrus the gentile king, who were instrumental in God's purposes in history, but there are also numerous accounts of those who had no special gifts or status, who also changed history by facilitating the plans of God, though we may never know their names.

More Possibilities
These are questions you might want to ask your students to help them put themselves into the skins of the people who lived these adventures:

—How was it to walk at night between the walls of water of the Red Sea…on dry land?

—What was it like when the quail came and God gave you your desire, but also leanness of soul?

—What was it like to wait with the baggage while David and the rest of the army went on without you?

—How would it have been to be blind Bartimeus, told to be quiet instead of cry out to Jesus for help?

—What would it be like to be the demon-possessed man, gashing himself with stones, so lost he had no hope, and tormented, and then to see Jesus coming specifically to you in the Gentile country of the Gadarenes? -What was it like in the upper room when tongues of fire sat on every head?

—What did Joseph think when he realized he would be responsible for bringing up the Messiah?

—What did the young Joseph (Genesis 29) think when the reward he got for doing right was to be thrown into a comfortless, miserable jail on false charges?

—How would it feel to be Demas, departing from the faith having loved this present world, or Archippus who needed encouragement to be not weary in well-doing, but to take heed to the ministry he had received in the Lord that he might fulfill it?

—What did Japeth think when God closed the door of the ark and he could hear the shouts outside as the rains began to fall?

—How would it have been to be a prisoner in the Philippian jail when Paul and Silas sang in the night? Or one of the elite Roman soldiers who had to spend a shift chained to Paul?

—and what about Malcus in the midst of with soldiers and torches, when Jesus picked up his severed ear, put it back on, and made him completely whole?

Living the Moment

Sometimes it's startling to follow a person in real time with all the unknowns and emotions rather than looking back knowing the whole story. We're so used to the Empty Tomb on Sunday morning that we might have a very hard time putting ourselves into the place of any of the followers of Jesus on Saturday.

My son, Thomas, was forty-eight when he emailed the following monologue to me on the Saturday between the crucifixion and the resurrection. It delighted me that, thirty years after leaving my class on writing biblical monologues, he still thinks about the people in the Bible and puts himself into their skins.

Mom,
It's Saturday and I woke up thinking about Peter and what he must have felt like early on Saturday morning.
Love,
Thomas

Peter On Saturday
by Thomas Ramirez

It's just like when I was walking on water. I knew I could stand with you, Jesus. We were in the garden and they came for us. I had a sword and took that guy's ear right off. I'd have taken them all out for you if you hadn't stopped me. We could have overthrown Rome right there. I mean, right ... there. We had them. I don't know what's wrong with you. Okay, I did figure out that the guys who came for us weren't the right guys. They weren't the really important ones so I followed like a super-spy. You were going to get to someone really high and then blast them. I knew what you were up to. I was ready. I was going to be right there. Okay, so John was going to be there too but, he's always hanging around and ... whatever ... I'm the one who took that guy's ear. I don't get why you put it back on but I'm sure you had a reason. Maybe you thought that guy would join our side when it all blew up. Yeah .. That's it.

I don't get it, Jesus. How could you do that to me? I've been following you for three years. Three years! I, I did miracles for you. I cast out demons, lots of demons. I could do anything. Well, there was that one demon that I couldn't handle, but the others couldn't handle it either. We were all in the same boat but they had never walked on water. That was just you and me. Just you and me. That was the coolest. I mean, you are so cool. You always know what to do. You went toe to toe with those big shot Pharisees. They thought they were sooo smart but you're just better. It was cool just hanging out with you when everyone else went home.

I know you were keeping track of me somehow. I mean, I was in the crowd, looking for my opening. Waiting for when I could jump in and save the day. I should have realized I was too popular and put on some disguise. You told me I'd deny you but I thought you were just telling me the plan. You know, I'm going to be brought before the magistrates, you're going to deny me. That's how we were going to get close to the leaders and then, Bam! We topple Rome. I know you didn't say it directly but you almost never say anything directly. We always have to figure it out. I'm still trying to figure out that Jonah thing. There's no fish here! I guess, there are probably some regular ones at the market and stuff. Were you going to turn one of those into a giant fish and it would swim you to safety? I don't get it.

So, Jesus, can you tell me why? Can you tell me why you just left me there? We were a team. I was going to rule with you. I was ready to die with you. I was ready to die for you. I was walking on water again, just you and me. No one else had figured it out. But when you looked at me. When you looked at me, I knew. I could see it in your eyes. I had messed up. I wasn't going to be a hero. I was just some idiot with a sword and you weren't going to save me this time. I could see the waves again and my feet started to sink but this time, this time you didn't catch me. This time you let me sink. This time you let me drown.

Who am I supposed to go to now? You are supposed to be the Christ. You have the words of life…

I'm so stupid! You gave us the power to heal. You gave us the power to raise the dead. That's it! Maybe there's one more chance. If I can find you. If I can get you away from the Sanhedrin… Who am I fooling? I can't do that. I don't understand your plan. I didn't even realize you were warning me, not telling me your plan. Why did you even bother with a stupid fisherman like me. You called me to walk on water and I couldn't even do that right. I don't even know why you tried to do anything with me. With any of us.

Comments from Thomas:
I like that it's so full of self and pride and crushing defeat with no hope in sight. He desperately needs to be enough to help Jesus, to be the hero but he has even failed as a sidekick.

At this point in time, Peter does not know if Jesus is alive or dead. After the third denial, Peter "went outside and wept bitterly." He doesn't know what will happen. He's just a mess and he doesn't even know where Jesus is or what he is going through. The Bible gives no clues as to what Peter does between when he goes outside and Sunday morning.

I love the desperate need to understand, to see how things fit together. This is definitely the "before" picture to Acts 4:13.

Love,
Thomas

Does It Need More?
Part of the art of writing is knowing when to stop. Does Peter's monologue need an epilogue? Maybe someone to say something about his reinstatement? Or is it more effective to leave it bleak and despairing, trusting that the audience will fill in what they know of the coming hours and days. Which will be more powerful? If you choose to use this monologue, you get to decide.

Dramatic Foundational Truth
Biblical monologues offer an opportunity to present basic foundational truth powerfully and dramatically. The Gospels tell of the suffering of our Lord Jesus Christ—His humiliation and the torture, but

because we become so familiar with the text, we can passively accept it as truth without letting it grip us in any meaningful way. A monologue from an eyewitness can effectively remind us of the severity of the price Jesus paid to redeem us, of our inestimable value to Him, and the immensity of our Father's love.

Joseph of Arimathea
by Carolyn Wing Greenlee

I cannot say it was easy to make the request after all I'd seen in the past forty-eight hours. The trial in the middle of the night, the lies, the railing accusations, the false witnesses—the unbelievable hatred poured out on one man…As the hours dragged on, it seemed increasingly to be a terrible nightmare, but rather than waking, I witnessed more depths of evil than I though possible from mere mortal man.

None of us had slept. Nicodemus and I felt angry and helpless. What could we do? We wanted to leave—to run away—to be anywhere else. But we couldn't move. We just kept watching—paralyzed, incredulous, uncomprehending as the whole horrible thing opened up before us—the beatings, the insults, the blasphemy, the humiliation. It was as if the devil himself mocked Him from every gaping human mouth. And then they sentenced Him. He seemed to glance in my direction. I was afraid to look lest anyone sense a connection between us. As they led Him away, I hid my face.

It was not easy seeing Him like that. I was angry, frightened. I wanted to defend Him—to shout His innocence against the lies—to shield Him from the blows. But I could not, and neither could Nicodemus. His jaw was set hard, the muscle in it tight. But we could not move. We could not speak. Few knew that we were secretly His disciples. The very thing for which they were condemning Him was the truth by which we had come to live: He was indeed the Son of God—our Messiah.

Three years I watched Him, listening skeptically, then eagerly to the reports about Him. I had been afraid to believe. But then I met Him. He reasoned with me from the Scriptures and light came into my mind. I understood God's wisdom, His goodness, His will, His way as never before. The vastness of His love overwhelmed me. The eyes of my understanding had been enlightened. I could not refuse the truth. My heart burned within me.

Why couldn't I so much as whisper in His defense? Was I ashamed? Of what? Of the answer I'd found to the emptiness in my life? Of the joy I found in His fellowship? Why was I afraid? Of what was I afraid? Of Man? He Himself declared we were not to fear Man. Man could only kill our bodies, but God could cast both body and soul into the everlasting torment of Gehenna.

I was ashamed, tormented. It was not just because I saw them beat Him. It was because I did nothing to stop it…nothing at all.

Then they murdered Him. We stood a long way off, Nicodemus and I—each one of us battling his own heart within him. It was over now. Perhaps things would return to normal…Perhaps no one would ever know that we had met with Him in secret and He had opened our lives with His eyes…We could go back to the synagogue and be respected and accepted, and no one would ever know . . .

It was hard to see because of the blackness of the sky. It was not simply dark—it was as if the darkness had weight and mass—a heaviness beyond night. I sensed the evil. My skin crawled. In the swirling dark, I could barely make out the forms of the soldiers breaking the legs of the thieves. I did not see them break His legs. I only saw His heavy limp form slung over the shoulder of the soldier who struggled to keep his balance on his way down the ladder while the black winds howled and lashed, whipping us all.

So many feelings surged inside! I ached from remorse and shame and grief. How I wished I could go back just hours before and do something—cry out in His defense, take the blows upon myself, suffer with Him, die with Him—something…anything but sit passively by… watching…silently.

Then they laid Him on the ground. I wanted to run to Him and wrap Him in something warm. He must be cold. (rueful laugh) That was foolish. He was dead. There was nothing to do but go home…go on with life. But how could I just leave Him there?

It was as if Nicodemus and I had the same thought at the same time. We could still do something. But the cost…the synagogue…our reputations…our wives and children…the safety of our own lives…

We watched them carry Him away.

Then, somehow, there I was, a prominent man of the synagogue feeling as insecure as a child while the governor pondered my request. His fingers drummed on the polished marble table. He was impatient, but after all he had seen, he was probably rather sickened by the whole matter. Then he gave the order and waved me away.

I had a fine linen cloth—the finest I could buy... I forced myself to think of Him cleanly washed and wrapped—the goal rather than the grim reality lying before me on the cold stone slab. If I had not watched from the time of the trial, I could not have believed it was He. Great raw wounds covered His jaw where a thick bushy beard had been. A battalion's worth of hateful fists battered His face deep blue. The cruel six-inch Jerusalem thorns they had beaten into His scalp seeped their poison till His face swelled to twice its normal size. His back...(bitterly) ha...there was nothing left of His back. His bones showed white and bloody where there was no skin or muscle left for the shard-laden whip to rip away. And where they had driven the spikes...

I do not know how I did it...the strength of God only. It was going to be Sabbath soon. Dusk was coming fast upon us. I hurried to warm the water, even though my mind knew He would not have felt the shock of the cold. Still, it hurt me to think of hurting Him. Every ragged edge of flesh rent me as I washed and rinsed and washed...all the dark, caked blood...every cruel raw wound—wounds for my transgressions. It made me angry as I washed and carefully dried the bruises—bruises for my iniquities. Nicodemus and I hurriedly sprinkled the myrrh and the aloes. It made me angry—that the chastisement of my peace was upon Him—that He bore my grief and my sorrow and my sin...and I esteemed Him not. I esteemed Him stricken, smitten by God and afflicted. I hid my face from Him. I, who had vowed to follow Him--I hid my face from Him! And the grief and the anger, the sorrow and the fury raged side by side as my tears slid down my beard and dropped on the ravaged flesh...on the fresh linen cloth. (He pauses, collects himself, and resumes speaking, but in a matter-of-fact tone.) I unfolded the napkin and carefully covered His face.

I did not know He would rise again. He had said, but we had not understood. When the women told us, it was like nonsense, like tales of their own imaginations. They were overcome with grieving. I was not surprised that they would say such things. I, too, longed to see Him again as He had been—strong and brown, with joy flashing in His eyes as He laughed with us at the table. But I knew, perhaps better than most, how very dead He was. Yes, I longed to see Him, but I did not hope. I had dressed the body. It did no good to hope. It only hurt.

But then He stood among us. I could almost not believe. When last I saw His face, it was…so different. The wounds, the ragged flesh. I could still see it when I closed my eyes. It had haunted my dreams. Yet there He was…shining. His eyes were shining. His face was shining.

I did not know, when I gathered my courage, forced away my fears of Man, and went before Pilate—I did not think, when I washed those wounds and wrapped His beloved face away behind the clean white cloth and listened to the grinding of stone against stone as the heavy door was rolled into its place—I did not expect, as I lay exhausted, yet sleepless upon my bed in the darkness which pervaded more than the night sky—I did not believe that He would be standing there amongst us, His eyes shining with forgiveness and acceptance that reached into Eternity. I did not do it for that. I only knew that He was my life and I could not deny Him any longer. Nothing else mattered any more.

My life has not been easier since that day. There are times when the Sanhedren is insanely vicious towards the Believers. There has already been much persecution, much suffering, many senseless and cruel deaths. Sometimes the days seem dark and dreadful indeed and fear seeks to grip me with talons of ice. Yet I remember the darkest time of all—when Satan seemed victorious, when hope and life itself seemed to lie ravaged in a hewn rock tomb…And then I remember His eyes…shining.

Last Thoughts

Many psalmists wrote, "The LORD is gracious in all His ways." Sometimes we just don't see how. Biblical monologues written with the insight gained by prayer can help us to better understand. We as Christians have the privilege to build our relationship with the One who saved us—to come to know Him in His true character, to understand the wisdom of His ways, to reveal Him in everything we do.

As we teach our children how to put themselves into the skins of biblical persons, we have the opportunity to help them gain spiritual insight into their actions, and into the reasons behind God's. We can then help bring them that understanding of God's goodness, mercy, and wisdom which develops in them the confidence that God is good always, and that the choice to surrender their lives to Him can bring nothing but fulfillment in the blessing of the Lord which makes rich and adds no sorrow.